Mastering Anxiety

Strategies for a Calmer Life

Willow R. Stone

Xspurts.com

A New Zealand Designed Product

Other Versions Available

Why limit yourself to just one format?

This book is now available in physical, digital, and audiobook options.

Choose the way you love to read and dive into the story today. You won't regret it!

Digital ISBN: 9781776968718
Physical ISBN: 9781776968701
Audio ISBN:

To obtain a different format of this book at a discounted price, please get in touch with us at:

http://isbn.xspurts.com/

Contents

Have Questions / Comments? 1

Get Free Stuff 3

1. Understanding Anxiety Disorders 5

2. Types of Anxiety Disorders 14

3. Specific Phobias 23

4. Causes and Risk Factors 29

5. Symptoms and Diagnosis 39

6. Comorbid Conditions 49

7. Treatment Options 64

8. Alternative and Complementary Treatments 75

9. Self-Help Strategies 87

10. Managing Panic Attacks 96

11. Overcoming Social Anxiety 104

12. Confronting Specific Phobias 111

13. Parenting a Child with Anxiety 118

14. Anxiety in Adolescents 125

15. Anxiety in the Workplace 133

16. Anxiety and Relationships 140

17. Women and Anxiety 148
18. Men and Anxiety 155
19. Aging and Anxiety 162
20. Anxiety and Technology 170
21. Coping with Health Anxiety 178
22. Resilience and Personal Growth 186
23. Sleep and Anxiety 199
24. Nutrition and Exercise 207
25. Creative Expression and Anxiety 214
26. Embracing Neurodiversity and Reducing Stigma 222
27. Resources and Support Networks 230
28. Personal Stories and Experiences 238

Have Questions / Comments?

This book was designed to cover as much information as possible, but I know I have probably missed something, or some new amazing discovery has just come out.

If you notice something missing or have a question that I failed to answer, please get in touch and let me know. If I can, I will email you an answer and also update the book so others can also benefit from it.

Thanks For Being Awesome :)

Submit Your Questions / Comments At:

https://questions.xspurts.com

Get Free Stuff

We love writing and have produced a huge number of books.

For being one of our amazing readers, we would love to offer you more books we have created, 100% free.

To claim this limited time special offer, simply go to the site below and enter your name and email address.

You will then receive loads (as we love our readers so much :) of our great books, content and audio direct to your email account, 100% free!

Get Loads of FREE Stuff at:

https://free.xspurts.com

Chapter One

Understanding Anxiety Disorders

Anxiety is a normal and natural emotion that everyone experiences from time to time. It's a feeling of unease, such as worry or fear, that can be mild or severe. But for some people, anxiety becomes an overwhelming force that interferes with their daily lives. Anxiety disorders are a group of mental health conditions that cause people to experience excessive and persistent anxiety, fear, or worry, often with no apparent reason.

Anxiety disorders are the most common mental health disorder in the United States, affecting about 18.1% of the population. While there is no one cause of anxiety disorders, research suggests that they can be caused by a combination of factors, including genetics, brain chemistry, personality, and life events.

There are several different types of anxiety disorders, each with its own set of symptoms and treatment options. Let's take a closer look at some of the most common types of anxiety disorders.

Generalized Anxiety Disorder (GAD)

Generalized Anxiety Disorder is a chronic condition characterized by excessive and persistent worry about everyday things. People with GAD tend to worry about everything from finances and health to work and relationships, often without any real cause for concern. The worry is often accompanied by physical symptoms, such as fatigue, muscle tension, and difficulty sleeping.

Panic Disorder

Panic Disorder is a type of anxiety disorder characterized by sudden and unexpected panic attacks. Panic attacks are intense episodes of fear and anxiety that can last anywhere from a few minutes to an hour. Symptoms of panic attacks include rapid heartbeat, sweating, trembling, chest pain, and difficulty breathing. Panic Disorder can be very disabling and can interfere with a person's ability to work, socialize, and enjoy life.

Social Anxiety Disorder

Social Anxiety Disorder is a type of anxiety disorder characterized by excessive fear or anxiety about social situations. People with social anxiety disorder often fear being judged or embarrassed in social situations, leading to avoidance of social events and isolation. Social anxiety disorder can be particularly challenging because it can affect a person's ability to form relationships, succeed in school or work, and enjoy life.

Obsessive-Compulsive Disorder (OCD)

Obsessive-Compulsive Disorder is a type of anxiety disorder characterized by intrusive and unwanted thoughts or images (obsessions) that lead to repetitive behaviors or mental acts (compulsions). People with OCD often feel that they must perform these behaviors in order to reduce their anxiety, even if they know that the behavior is irrational or excessive. OCD can be very time-consuming and can interfere with a person's ability to work, socialize, and enjoy life.

Post-Traumatic Stress Disorder (PTSD)

Post-Traumatic Stress Disorder is a type of anxiety disorder that can develop after experiencing or witnessing a traumatic event. People with PTSD often re-experience the traumatic event through flashbacks, nightmares, or intrusive thoughts. They may also avoid situations or people that remind them of the traumatic event and may feel numb or detached from their surroundings. PTSD can be very disabling and can interfere with a person's ability to work, socialize, and enjoy life.

Treatment for Anxiety Disorders

Fortunately, anxiety disorders are treatable, and most people with anxiety disorders can lead healthy and productive lives with proper treatment. Treatment options for anxiety disorders include medication, therapy, or a combination of both.

Medications used to treat anxiety disorders include antidepressants, anti-anxiety medications, and beta-blockers. These medications can help reduce the symptoms of anxiety and help people manage their anxiety more effectively.

Therapy for anxiety disorders can take many forms, including cognitive-behavioral therapy (CBT), exposure therapy, and mindfulness-based therapy. CBT is a type of therapy that helps people identify and change negative patterns of thought and behavior that contribute to anxiety. Exposure therapy is a type of therapy that helps

Defining anxiety and its different manifestations

Anxiety is a natural human response to stress or danger. It is a feeling of apprehension or fear about what may happen in the future. While some level of anxiety is normal, for some people, anxiety can become overwhelming and interfere with their daily lives. Anxiety disorders are a group of mental health conditions that cause people to experience excessive and persistent anxiety, fear, or worry, often with no apparent reason.

Anxiety disorders are the most common mental health disorders in the United States, affecting about 18.1% of the population. While there is no one cause of anxiety disorders, research suggests that they can be caused by a combination of factors, including genetics, brain chemistry, personality, and life events.

There are several different types of anxiety disorders, each with its own set of symptoms and treatment options. Let's take a closer look at some of the most common types of anxiety disorders.

Generalized Anxiety Disorder (GAD)

Generalized Anxiety Disorder is a chronic condition characterized by excessive and persistent worry about everyday things. People with GAD tend to worry about everything from finances and health to work and relationships, often without any real cause for concern. The worry is often accompanied by physical symptoms, such as fatigue, muscle tension, and difficulty sleeping.

Panic Disorder

Panic Disorder is a type of anxiety disorder characterized by sudden and unexpected panic attacks. Panic attacks are intense episodes of fear and anxiety that can last anywhere from a few minutes to an hour. Symptoms of panic attacks include rapid heartbeat, sweating, trembling, chest pain, and difficulty breathing. Panic Disorder can be very disabling and can interfere with a person's ability to work, socialize, and enjoy life.

Social Anxiety Disorder

Social Anxiety Disorder is a type of anxiety disorder characterized by excessive fear or anxiety about social situations. People with social anxiety disorder often fear being judged or embarrassed in social situations, leading to avoidance of social events and isolation. Social anxiety disorder can be particularly challenging because it can affect a person's ability to form relationships, succeed in school or work, and enjoy life.

Obsessive-Compulsive Disorder (OCD)

Obsessive-Compulsive Disorder is a type of anxiety disorder characterized by intrusive and unwanted thoughts or images (obsessions) that lead to repetitive behaviors or mental acts (compulsions). People with OCD often feel that they must perform these behaviors in order to reduce their anxiety, even if they know that the behavior is irrational or excessive. OCD can be very time-consuming and can interfere with a person's ability to work, socialize, and enjoy life.

Post-Traumatic Stress Disorder (PTSD)

Post-Traumatic Stress Disorder is a type of anxiety disorder that can develop after experiencing or witnessing a traumatic event. People with PTSD often re-experience the traumatic event through flashbacks, nightmares, or intrusive thoughts. They may also avoid situations or people that remind them of the traumatic event and may feel numb or detached from their surroundings. PTSD can be very disabling and can interfere with a person's ability to work, socialize, and enjoy life.

Agoraphobia

Agoraphobia is a type of anxiety disorder characterized by a fear of being in situations where escape may be difficult or embarrassing, or where help may not be available in case of a panic attack or other physical symptoms. People with agoraphobia may avoid going to public places, such as shopping malls, crowded restaurants, or public transportation, and may become isolated as a result.

Specific Phobias

Specific Phobias are a type of anxiety disorder characterized by a persistent and irrational fear of a specific object, situation, or activity. Common phobias include heights, spiders, flying, and enclosed spaces. People with specific phobias may avoid the object or situation that triggers their fear, leading to disruption of daily

The role of the fight-or-flight response

The fight-or-flight response is a natural physiological reaction that occurs in response to a perceived threat. It is a survival mechanism that prepares the body to either fight the threat or flee from it. The fight-or-flight response is a complex process that involves several physiological systems working together to prepare the body for action.

When a threat is perceived, the amygdala, a small almond-shaped structure in the brain, sends a signal to the hypothalamus, which activates the sympathetic nervous system. The sympathetic nervous system then triggers the release of adrenaline and other stress hormones, which cause several changes in the body.

The heart rate increases, blood pressure rises, and breathing becomes more rapid and shallow. The blood vessels in the skin constrict, diverting blood flow to the major muscles of the body, which become tense and ready for action. The pupils dilate, allowing more light to enter the eyes, and the digestive system slows down, diverting energy to the muscles.

All of these changes are designed to prepare the body to either fight the threat or flee from it. The fight-or-flight response can be a helpful and necessary response to a dangerous situation. However, in people with anxiety disorders, the fight-or-flight response can become triggered in situations that are not actually dangerous, leading to excessive and persistent anxiety, fear, or worry.

For example, in people with social anxiety disorder, the fight-or-flight response may be triggered in social situations, leading to excessive fear and avoidance of social events. In people with panic disorder, the fight-or-flight response may be triggered by a perceived threat of a panic attack, leading to intense anxiety and panic.

The fight-or-flight response can also be triggered by traumatic events, leading to the development of post-traumatic stress disorder (PTSD). In people with PTSD, the fight-or-flight response may be triggered by reminders of the traumatic event, leading to flashbacks, nightmares, and other symptoms.

While the fight-or-flight response is a natural and necessary response to danger, excessive or persistent activation of the response can lead to the development of anxiety disorders. Understanding the role of the fight-or-flight response in anxiety disorders is an important step in developing effective treatments for these conditions.

One approach to treating anxiety disorders is to target the physiological systems involved in the fight-or-flight response. Medications such as beta-blockers can be used to block the effects of adrenaline and other stress hormones, reducing the physical symptoms of anxiety.

Another approach is to use cognitive-behavioral therapy (CBT) to help people with anxiety disorders learn to identify and challenge their anxious thoughts and beliefs. By changing the way they think about and respond to perceived threats, people with anxiety disorders can learn to reduce the activation of the fight-or-flight response.

Mindfulness-based therapies, such as mindfulness-based stress reduction (MBSR), can also be effective in reducing the activation of the fight-or-flight response. By learning to focus on the present moment and observe their thoughts and emotions without judgment, people with anxiety disorders can learn to reduce the intensity and frequency of the fight-or-flight response.

Prevalence and impact of anxiety disorders

Anxiety disorders are a group of mental health conditions that cause people to experience excessive and persistent anxiety, fear, or worry, often with no apparent reason. These disorders are the most common mental health disorders in the United States, affecting about 18.1% of the population.

Anxiety disorders can be caused by a combination of factors, including genetics, brain chemistry, personality, and life events. They can be disabling and can interfere with a person's ability to work, socialize, and enjoy life. Let's take a closer look at the prevalence and impact of anxiety disorders.

Prevalence of Anxiety Disorders

Anxiety disorders are the most common mental health disorders in the United States, affecting about 18.1% of the population. They are more common in women than in men, and they can occur at any age. Anxiety disorders often co-occur with other mental health disorders, such as depression or substance abuse.

Some specific types of anxiety disorders are more common than others. Generalized Anxiety Disorder (GAD) is the most common anxiety disorder, affecting about 6.8 million adults in the United States. Panic Disorder affects about 6 million adults, Social Anxiety Disorder affects about 15 million adults, and Obsessive-Compulsive Disorder (OCD) affects about 2.2 million adults.

Impact of Anxiety Disorders

Anxiety disorders can have a significant impact on a person's life. They can interfere with a person's ability to work, socialize, and enjoy life. Anxiety disorders can also lead to physical symptoms, such as fatigue, muscle tension, and difficulty sleeping.

Anxiety disorders can also lead to other mental health problems. For example, people with anxiety disorders are at increased risk for developing depression or substance abuse. Anxiety disorders can also increase the risk of suicidal thoughts and behaviors.

Anxiety disorders can also have an economic impact. People with anxiety disorders often miss work or school due to their symptoms, which can lead to decreased productivity and income. Anxiety disorders can also lead to increased healthcare costs, as people with anxiety disorders often require medical care to manage their symptoms.

Treatment of Anxiety Disorders

Fortunately, anxiety disorders are treatable, and most people with anxiety disorders can lead healthy and productive lives with proper treatment. Treatment options for anxiety disorders include medication, therapy, or a combination of both.

Medications used to treat anxiety disorders include antidepressants, anti-anxiety medications, and beta-blockers. These medications can help reduce the symptoms of anxiety and help people manage their anxiety more effectively.

Therapy for anxiety disorders can take many forms, including cognitive-behavioral therapy (CBT), exposure therapy, and mindfulness-based therapy. CBT is a type of therapy that helps people identify and change negative patterns of thought and behavior that contribute to anxiety. Exposure therapy is a type of therapy that helps people gradually face their fears and anxieties in a safe and controlled environment, helping to reduce the intensity of their anxiety over time. Mindfulness-based therapies can help people learn to focus on the present moment and observe their thoughts and emotions without judgment, reducing the intensity and frequency of their anxiety over time.

Chapter Two

Types of Anxiety Disorders

Anxiety is a natural human emotion that everyone experiences from time to time. It is a feeling of unease, such as worry or fear, that can be mild or severe. However, for some people, anxiety can become overwhelming and interfere with their daily lives. Anxiety disorders are a group of mental health conditions that cause people to experience excessive and persistent anxiety, fear, or worry, often with no apparent reason. There are several different types of anxiety disorders, each with its own set of symptoms and treatment options. Let's take a closer look at some of the most common types of anxiety disorders.

Generalized Anxiety Disorder (GAD)

Generalized Anxiety Disorder is a chronic condition characterized by excessive and persistent worry about everyday things. People with GAD tend to worry about everything from finances and health to work and relationships, often without any real cause for concern. The worry is often accompanied by physical symptoms, such as fatigue, muscle tension, and difficulty sleeping.

Panic Disorder

Panic Disorder is a type of anxiety disorder characterized by sudden and unexpected panic attacks. Panic attacks are intense episodes of fear and anxiety that can last anywhere from a few minutes to an hour. Symptoms of panic attacks include rapid heartbeat, sweating, trembling, chest pain, and difficulty breathing. Panic Disorder can be very disabling and can interfere with a person's ability to work, socialize, and enjoy life.

Social Anxiety Disorder

Social Anxiety Disorder is a type of anxiety disorder characterized by excessive fear or anxiety about social situations. People with social anxiety disorder often fear being judged or embarrassed in social situations, leading to avoidance of social events and isolation. Social anxiety disorder can be particularly challenging because it can affect a person's ability to form relationships, succeed in school or work, and enjoy life.

Obsessive-Compulsive Disorder (OCD)

Obsessive-Compulsive Disorder is a type of anxiety disorder characterized by intrusive and unwanted thoughts or images (obsessions) that lead to repetitive behaviors or mental acts (compulsions). People with OCD often feel that they must perform these behaviors in order to reduce their anxiety, even if they know that the behavior is irrational or excessive. OCD can be very time-consuming and can interfere with a person's ability to work, socialize, and enjoy life.

Post-Traumatic Stress Disorder (PTSD)

Post-Traumatic Stress Disorder is a type of anxiety disorder that can develop after experiencing or witnessing a traumatic event. People with PTSD often re-experience the traumatic event through flashbacks, nightmares, or intrusive thoughts. They may also avoid situations or people that remind them of the traumatic event and may feel numb or detached from their surroundings. PTSD can be very disabling and can interfere with a person's ability to work, socialize, and enjoy life.

Agoraphobia

Agoraphobia is a type of anxiety disorder characterized by a fear of being in situations where escape may be difficult or embarrassing, or where help may not be available in case of a panic attack or other physical symptoms. People with agoraphobia may avoid going to public places, such as shopping malls, crowded restaurants, or public transportation, and may become isolated as a result.

Specific Phobias

Specific Phobias are a type of anxiety disorder characterized by a persistent and irrational fear of a specific object, situation, or activity. Common phobias include heights, spiders, flying, and enclosed spaces. People with specific phobias may avoid the object or situation that triggers their fear, leading to disruption of daily activities.

Separation Anxiety Disorder

Separation Anxiety Disorder is a type of anxiety disorder that is commonly diagnosed in children but can also occur in adults. It is characterized by excessive and persistent anxiety about separation from a person or place that provides a sense of security or comfort. People with separation anxiety disorder may

Generalized Anxiety Disorder (GAD)

Generalized Anxiety Disorder (GAD) is a chronic condition characterized by excessive and persistent worry about everyday things. People with GAD tend to worry about everything from finances and health to work and relationships, often without any real cause for concern. The worry is often accompanied by physical symptoms, such as fatigue, muscle tension, and difficulty sleeping.

Symptoms of Generalized Anxiety Disorder

The symptoms of GAD can be both physical and psychological. Physical symptoms may include fatigue, muscle tension, headaches, difficulty sleeping, and gastrointestinal problems. Psychological symptoms may include excessive worry, irritability, restlessness, difficulty concentrating, and difficulty controlling worry.

People with GAD may also experience symptoms of other anxiety disorders, such as panic attacks or social anxiety, as well as symptoms of depression. GAD can be a very debilitating condition that can interfere with a person's ability to work, socialize, and enjoy life.

Causes of Generalized Anxiety Disorder

The exact causes of GAD are not fully understood, but it is likely that a combination of factors, including genetics, brain chemistry, personality, and life events, contribute to the development of the disorder.

Studies have shown that people with GAD may have imbalances in certain chemicals in the brain, such as serotonin and norepinephrine, which are involved in regulating mood and anxiety. Genetics may also play a role in the development of GAD, as it tends to run in families.

Personality traits, such as perfectionism and a tendency to worry excessively, may also contribute to the development of GAD. Life events, such as traumatic experiences or chronic stress, may also trigger the onset of GAD.

Treatment of Generalized Anxiety Disorder

Fortunately, GAD is a treatable condition. Treatment options for GAD include medication, therapy, or a combination of both.

Medications used to treat GAD include antidepressants, anti-anxiety medications, and beta-blockers. These medications can help reduce the symptoms of anxiety and help people manage their anxiety more effectively.

Therapy for GAD can take many forms, including cognitive-behavioral therapy (CBT), exposure therapy, and mindfulness-based therapy. CBT is a type of therapy that helps people identify and change negative patterns of thought and behavior that contribute to anxiety. Exposure therapy is a type of therapy that helps people gradually face their fears and anxieties in a safe and controlled environment, helping to reduce the intensity of their anxiety over time. Mindfulness-based therapies can help people learn to focus on the present moment and observe their thoughts and emotions without judgment, reducing the intensity and frequency of their anxiety over time.

Self-care strategies can also be helpful in managing GAD. These strategies may include exercise, relaxation techniques, such as deep breathing or meditation, and self-care activities, such as spending time with loved ones or engaging in hobbies.

Panic Disorder

Panic Disorder is a type of anxiety disorder characterized by sudden and unexpected panic attacks. Panic attacks are intense episodes of fear and anxiety that can last anywhere from a few minutes to an hour. Symptoms of panic attacks include rapid heartbeat, sweating, trembling, chest pain, and difficulty breathing. Panic Disorder can be very disabling and can interfere with a person's ability to work, socialize, and enjoy life.

Symptoms of Panic Disorder

The symptoms of Panic Disorder can be both physical and psychological. Physical symptoms may include rapid heartbeat, sweating, trembling, chest pain, shortness of breath, dizziness, and nausea. Psychological symptoms may include intense fear, a feeling of impending doom or danger, and a sense of being out of control.

People with Panic Disorder may also experience symptoms of other anxiety disorders, such as Generalized Anxiety Disorder (GAD) or social anxiety, as well as symptoms of depression. Panic Disorder can be a very debilitating condition that can interfere with a person's ability to work, socialize, and enjoy life.

Causes of Panic Disorder

The exact causes of Panic Disorder are not fully understood, but it is likely that a combination of factors, including genetics, brain chemistry, personality, and life events, contribute to the development of the disorder.

Studies have shown that people with Panic Disorder may have imbalances in certain chemicals in the brain, such as serotonin and norepinephrine, which are involved in regulating mood and anxiety. Genetics may also play a role in the development of Panic Disorder, as it tends to run in families.

Personality traits, such as a tendency to worry excessively or a tendency to be highly sensitive to stress, may also contribute to the development of Panic Disorder. Life events, such as a traumatic experience or chronic stress, may also trigger the onset of Panic Disorder.

Treatment of Panic Disorder

Fortunately, Panic Disorder is a treatable condition. Treatment options for Panic Disorder include medication, therapy, or a combination of both.

Medications used to treat Panic Disorder include antidepressants, anti-anxiety medications, and beta-blockers. These medications can help reduce the symptoms of anxiety and help people manage their anxiety more effectively.

Therapy for Panic Disorder can take many forms, including cognitive-behavioral therapy (CBT), exposure therapy, and relaxation techniques. CBT is a type of therapy that helps people identify and change negative patterns of thought and behavior that contribute to anxiety. Exposure therapy is a type of therapy that helps people gradually face their fears and anxieties in a safe and controlled environment, helping to reduce the intensity of their anxiety over time. Relaxation techniques, such as deep breathing or meditation, can also be helpful in managing Panic Disorder.

Self-care strategies can also be helpful in managing Panic Disorder. These strategies may include exercise, avoiding caffeine and other stimulants, getting enough sleep, and avoiding drugs and alcohol.

Social Anxiety Disorder

Social Anxiety Disorder is a type of anxiety disorder characterized by excessive fear or anxiety about social situations. People with social anxiety disorder often fear being judged or embarrassed in social situations, leading to avoidance of social events and isolation. Social anxiety disorder can be particularly challenging because it can affect a person's ability to form relationships, succeed in school or work, and enjoy life.

Symptoms of Social Anxiety Disorder

The symptoms of Social Anxiety Disorder can be both physical and psychological. Physical symptoms may include sweating, trembling, blushing, nausea, and difficulty breathing. Psychological symptoms may include fear of being judged or criticized, fear of embarrassing oneself in front of others, and fear of being the center of attention.

People with Social Anxiety Disorder may also experience symptoms of other anxiety disorders, such as Generalized Anxiety Disorder (GAD) or Panic Disorder, as well as symptoms of depression. Social Anxiety Disorder can be a very debilitating condition that can interfere with a person's ability to work, socialize, and enjoy life.

Causes of Social Anxiety Disorder

The exact causes of Social Anxiety Disorder are not fully understood, but it is likely that a combination of factors, including genetics, brain chemistry, personality, and life events, contribute to the development of the disorder.

Studies have shown that people with Social Anxiety Disorder may have imbalances in certain chemicals in the brain, such as serotonin and norepinephrine, which are involved in regulating mood and anxiety. Genetics may also play a role in the development of Social Anxiety Disorder, as it tends to run in families.

Personality traits, such as shyness, low self-esteem, and a tendency to worry excessively, may also contribute to the development of Social Anxiety Disorder. Life events, such as a traumatic experience or chronic stress, may also trigger the onset of Social Anxiety Disorder.

Treatment of Social Anxiety Disorder

Fortunately, Social Anxiety Disorder is a treatable condition. Treatment options for Social Anxiety Disorder include medication, therapy, or a combination of both.

Medications used to treat Social Anxiety Disorder include antidepressants and anti-anxiety medications. These medications can help reduce the symptoms of anxiety and help people manage their anxiety more effectively.

Therapy for Social Anxiety Disorder can take many forms, including cognitive-behavioral therapy (CBT), exposure therapy, and social skills training. CBT is a type of therapy that helps people identify and change negative patterns of thought and behavior that contribute to anxiety. Exposure therapy is a type of therapy that helps people gradually face their fears and anxieties in a safe and controlled environment, helping to reduce the intensity of their anxiety over time. Social skills training can help people learn how to interact with others in a more comfortable and confident way.

Self-care strategies can also be helpful in managing Social Anxiety Disorder. These strategies may include exercise, relaxation techniques, such as deep breathing or meditation, and self-care activities, such as spending time with loved ones or engaging in hobbies.

Chapter Three

Specific Phobias

Specific Phobias are a type of anxiety disorder characterized by intense and irrational fear of a particular object, situation, or activity. People with specific phobias often go to great lengths to avoid the object of their fear, leading to significant impairment in their daily lives. Specific phobias are different from other anxiety disorders in that the fear is focused on a specific object or situation rather than a general feeling of anxiety.

Symptoms of Specific Phobias

The symptoms of Specific Phobias can be both physical and psychological. Physical symptoms may include sweating, trembling, rapid heartbeat, difficulty breathing, and nausea. Psychological symptoms may include intense fear, a feeling of being out of control, and a sense of impending danger.

Specific Phobias can be focused on a wide range of objects or situations, including animals, heights, blood, flying, and enclosed spaces. The fear is often out of proportion to the actual danger posed by the object or situation.

Causes of Specific Phobias

The exact causes of Specific Phobias are not fully understood, but it is likely that a combination of factors, including genetics, brain chemistry, personality, and life events, contribute to the development of the disorder.

Studies have shown that people with Specific Phobias may have imbalances in certain chemicals in the brain, such as serotonin and norepinephrine, which are involved in regulating mood and anxiety. Genetics may also play a role in the development of Specific Phobias, as they tend to run in families.

Life events, such as a traumatic experience, may also trigger the onset of Specific Phobias. For example, a person who was bitten by a dog as a child may develop a specific phobia of dogs.

Treatment of Specific Phobias

Fortunately, Specific Phobias are a treatable condition. Treatment options for Specific Phobias include therapy, medication, or a combination of both.

Therapy for Specific Phobias can take many forms, including cognitive-behavioral therapy (CBT), exposure therapy, and desensitization therapy. CBT is a type of therapy that helps people identify and change negative patterns of thought and behavior that contribute to anxiety. Exposure therapy is a type of therapy that helps people gradually face their fears and anxieties in a safe and controlled environment, helping to reduce the intensity of their anxiety over time. Desensitization therapy is a type of therapy that involves exposing people to the object of their fear in a gradual and controlled manner, helping them to overcome their fear.

Medications used to treat Specific Phobias include anti-anxiety medications and beta-blockers. These medications can help reduce the symptoms of anxiety and help people manage their anxiety more effectively.

Self-care strategies can also be helpful in managing Specific Phobias. These strategies may include exercise, relaxation techniques, such as deep breathing or meditation, and self-care activities, such as spending time with loved ones or engaging in hobbies.

Separation Anxiety Disorder

Separation Anxiety Disorder is a type of anxiety disorder that occurs when a person experiences excessive and persistent anxiety about being separated from their home or from people they are attached to. Separation Anxiety Disorder is most commonly seen in children, but can also affect adults.

Symptoms of Separation Anxiety Disorder

The symptoms of Separation Anxiety Disorder can be both physical and psychological. Physical symptoms may include headaches, stomach aches, and nausea. Psychological symptoms may include excessive worry about separation from loved ones, fear of harm to loved ones, and difficulty sleeping alone.

Children with Separation Anxiety Disorder may also experience nightmares, clinginess, and tantrums when faced with separation from their primary caregiver. They may also refuse to attend school or other activities that require separation from their primary caregiver.

Causes of Separation Anxiety Disorder

The exact causes of Separation Anxiety Disorder are not fully understood, but it is likely that a combination of factors, including genetics, brain chemistry, personality, and life events, contribute to the development of the disorder.

Studies have shown that people with Separation Anxiety Disorder may have imbalances in certain chemicals in the brain, such as serotonin and norepinephrine, which are involved in regulating mood and anxiety. Genetics may also play a role in the development of Separation Anxiety Disorder, as it tends to run in families.

Life events, such as a traumatic experience or a major life change, may also trigger the onset of Separation Anxiety Disorder.

Treatment of Separation Anxiety Disorder

Fortunately, Separation Anxiety Disorder is a treatable condition. Treatment options for Separation Anxiety Disorder include therapy, medication, or a combination of both.

Therapy for Separation Anxiety Disorder can take many forms, including cognitive-behavioral therapy (CBT), family therapy, and play therapy. CBT is a type of therapy that helps people identify and change negative patterns of thought and behavior that contribute to anxiety. Family therapy can help families learn coping strategies and improve communication to better manage the child's anxiety. Play therapy can help children learn to express their feelings in a safe and comfortable environment.

Medications used to treat Separation Anxiety Disorder include antidepressants and anti-anxiety medications. These medications can help reduce the symptoms of anxiety and help people manage their anxiety more effectively.

Self-care strategies can also be helpful in managing Separation Anxiety Disorder. These strategies may include exercise, relaxation techniques, such as deep breathing or meditation, and self-care activities, such as spending time with loved ones or engaging in hobbies.

Agoraphobia

Agoraphobia is a type of anxiety disorder characterized by intense fear or anxiety about being in situations where escape might be difficult or help might not be available in the event of a panic attack or other anxiety symptoms. People with agoraphobia often avoid certain places or situations, which can greatly limit their ability to function in daily life.

Symptoms of Agoraphobia

The symptoms of Agoraphobia can be both physical and psychological. Physical symptoms may include sweating, trembling, rapid heartbeat, difficulty breathing, and nausea. Psychological symptoms may include fear of being in enclosed spaces, fear of being in open spaces, fear of being in crowds or public places, and fear of being alone.

People with Agoraphobia may also experience symptoms of other anxiety disorders, such as Generalized Anxiety Disorder (GAD) or Panic Disorder, as well as symptoms of depression. Agoraphobia can be a very debilitating condition that can interfere with a person's ability to work, socialize, and enjoy life.

Causes of Agoraphobia

The exact causes of Agoraphobia are not fully understood, but it is likely that a combination of factors, including genetics, brain chemistry, personality, and life events, contribute to the development of the disorder.

Studies have shown that people with Agoraphobia may have imbalances in certain chemicals in the brain, such as serotonin and norepinephrine, which are involved in regulating mood and anxiety. Genetics may also play a role in the development of Agoraphobia, as it tends to run in families.

Personality traits, such as shyness, low self-esteem, and a tendency to worry excessively, may also contribute to the development of Agoraphobia. Life events, such as a traumatic experience or chronic stress, may also trigger the onset of Agoraphobia.

Treatment of Agoraphobia

Fortunately, Agoraphobia is a treatable condition. Treatment options for Agoraphobia include therapy, medication, or a combination of both.

Therapy for Agoraphobia can take many forms, including cognitive-behavioral therapy (CBT), exposure therapy, and relaxation techniques. CBT is a type of therapy that helps people identify and change negative patterns of thought and behavior that contribute to anxiety. Exposure therapy is a type of therapy that helps people gradually face their fears and anxieties in a safe and controlled environment, helping to reduce the intensity of their anxiety over time. Relaxation techniques, such as deep breathing or meditation, can also be helpful in managing the symptoms of Agoraphobia.

Medications used to treat Agoraphobia include antidepressants and anti-anxiety medications. These medications can help reduce the symptoms of anxiety and help people manage their anxiety more effectively.

Self-care strategies can also be helpful in managing Agoraphobia. These strategies may include exercise, relaxation techniques, such as deep breathing or meditation, and self-care activities, such as spending time with loved ones or engaging in hobbies.

Chapter Four

Causes and Risk Factors

Anxiety disorders are a group of mental health conditions that are characterized by excessive and persistent worry or fear. Anxiety disorders can be caused by a variety of factors, including genetics, brain chemistry, environmental factors, and life events. Below we will explore the causes and risk factors associated with anxiety disorders.

Genetics

Studies have shown that genetics may play a role in the development of anxiety disorders. People with a family history of anxiety disorders are more likely to develop the condition themselves. Research has identified specific genes that may be associated with the development of anxiety disorders.

Brain Chemistry

Anxiety disorders are also believed to be caused by imbalances in certain chemicals in the brain, such as serotonin and norepinephrine, which are involved in regulating mood and anxiety. Imbalances in these chemicals can lead to heightened levels of anxiety.

Environmental Factors

Environmental factors can also play a role in the development of anxiety disorders. Traumatic experiences, such as physical or emotional abuse, can trigger the onset of anxiety disorders. Chronic stress, such as job stress or financial stress, can also contribute to the development of anxiety disorders.

Life Events

Life events, such as major life changes or transitions, can also trigger the onset of anxiety disorders. Moving to a new city, starting a new job, or going through a divorce can all be stressful events that can lead to the development of anxiety disorders.

Risk Factors

Certain factors can increase a person's risk of developing anxiety disorders. These risk factors include:

1. Family history: People with a family history of anxiety disorders are more likely to develop the condition themselves.

2. Gender: Women are more likely to develop anxiety disorders than men.

3. Personality: People with certain personality traits, such as perfectionism, pessimism, and a tendency to worry excessively, may be more susceptible to developing anxiety disorders.

4. Trauma: People who have experienced trauma, such as physical or emotional abuse, are more likely to develop anxiety disorders.

5. Chronic Stress: People who experience chronic stress, such as job stress or financial stress, are more likely to develop anxiety disorders.

6. Medical Conditions: People with certain medical conditions, such as heart disease, diabetes, or thyroid problems, may be at an increased risk for developing anxiety disorders.

Genetic and biological factors

Anxiety disorders are a group of mental health conditions that are characterized by excessive and persistent worry or fear. While the exact causes of anxiety disorders are not fully understood, genetic and biological factors are believed to play a significant role in the development of these conditions.

Genetic Factors

Studies have shown that genetics may play a role in the development of anxiety disorders. People with a family history of anxiety disorders are more likely to develop the condition themselves. Research has identified specific genes that may be associated with the development of anxiety disorders.

One study found that a gene called COMT, which is involved in the regulation of dopamine, a neurotransmitter that plays a role in anxiety, may be linked to the development of anxiety disorders. Another study found that a gene called BDNF, which is involved in the growth and maintenance of brain cells, may be associated with the development of anxiety disorders.

While genetic factors may increase a person's risk of developing anxiety disorders, it is important to note that not all people with a family history of anxiety disorders will develop the condition themselves. Other factors, such as environmental factors and life events, can also play a role in the development of anxiety disorders.

Biological Factors

Anxiety disorders are also believed to be caused by imbalances in certain chemicals in the brain, such as serotonin and norepinephrine, which are involved in regulating mood and anxiety. Imbalances in these chemicals can lead to heightened levels of anxiety.

Research has also shown that the amygdala, a part of the brain that is involved in processing emotions, may be overactive in people with anxiety disorders. This overactivity may contribute to heightened levels of anxiety.

In addition, the hypothalamic-pituitary-adrenal (HPA) axis, which is involved in the body's stress response, may be dysregulated in people with anxiety disorders. This dysregulation can lead to increased levels of the stress hormone cortisol, which can contribute to anxiety.

Treatment Implications

Understanding the genetic and biological factors involved in the development of anxiety disorders can help inform treatment approaches. For example, medications that target specific neurotransmitters, such as serotonin and norepinephrine, can be effective in reducing anxiety symptoms.

Cognitive-behavioral therapy (CBT) is another effective treatment approach for anxiety disorders. CBT focuses on identifying and changing negative patterns of thought and behavior that contribute to anxiety. By learning new coping strategies and changing negative thought patterns, people with anxiety disorders can learn to manage their symptoms more effectively.

Other treatment approaches for anxiety disorders may include relaxation techniques, such as deep breathing or meditation, and exposure therapy, which involves gradually exposing a person to feared situations in a safe and controlled environment.

Environmental influences

While genetic and biological factors are believed to play a significant role in the development of anxiety disorders, environmental influences can also contribute to the onset of these conditions. Below we will explore the environmental factors that can contribute to the development of anxiety disorders.

Trauma

Trauma is a significant environmental factor that can contribute to the development of anxiety disorders. Physical or emotional abuse, neglect, or witnessing violence can all be traumatic experiences that can trigger the onset of anxiety disorders. People who have experienced trauma may be more likely to develop post-traumatic stress disorder (PTSD), which is a type of anxiety disorder.

Chronic Stress

Chronic stress is another environmental factor that can contribute to the development of anxiety disorders. Chronic stress can come from a variety of sources, such as job stress, financial stress, or relationship stress. Over time, chronic stress can take a toll on a person's mental health and contribute to the onset of anxiety disorders.

Life Events

Life events, such as major life changes or transitions, can also trigger the onset of anxiety disorders. Moving to a new city, starting a new job, or going through a divorce can all be stressful events that can lead to the development of anxiety disorders.

Parenting Style

Parenting style can also contribute to the development of anxiety disorders. Children who are raised by overprotective or controlling parents may be more likely to develop anxiety disorders. Overprotective parents may inadvertently communicate to their children that the world is a dangerous place and that they need to be constantly on guard. This can contribute to heightened levels of anxiety in children.

Cultural and Societal Factors

Cultural and societal factors can also contribute to the development of anxiety disorders. In some cultures, there may be a stigma associated with mental health conditions, which can make it difficult for people to seek treatment for anxiety disorders. Societal factors, such as increased exposure to violence or social media, can also contribute to heightened levels of anxiety.

Treatment Implications

Understanding the environmental factors that can contribute to the development of anxiety disorders can help inform treatment approaches. For example, trauma-focused therapy can be effective in treating PTSD, which is a type of anxiety disorder that can be triggered by traumatic experiences.

Cognitive-behavioral therapy (CBT) is another effective treatment approach for anxiety disorders that may be related to chronic stress, life events, or parenting style. CBT focuses on identifying and changing negative patterns of thought and behavior that contribute to anxiety. By learning new coping strategies and changing negative thought patterns, people with anxiety disorders can learn to manage their symptoms more effectively.

Other treatment approaches for anxiety disorders may include relaxation techniques, such as deep breathing or meditation, and exposure therapy, which involves gradually exposing a person to feared situations in a safe and controlled environment.

Personality traits and temperament

Personality traits and temperament can also play a role in the development of anxiety disorders. Below we will explore how personality traits and temperament can contribute to the onset of anxiety disorders.

Perfectionism

Perfectionism is a personality trait that involves setting high standards for oneself and striving for perfection in all aspects of life. While perfectionism can be a positive trait, it can also contribute to the development of anxiety disorders. People who are perfectionists may be more prone to worry and self-doubt, which can contribute to heightened levels of anxiety.

Pessimism

Pessimism is another personality trait that can contribute to the development of anxiety disorders. People who are pessimistic tend to have a negative outlook on life and may view the world as a dangerous and threatening place. This negative outlook can contribute to heightened levels of anxiety.

Worrying

Excessive worrying is a common symptom of anxiety disorders, but it can also be a personality trait that contributes to the development of these conditions. People who are chronic worriers may be more likely to develop anxiety disorders. This is because excessive worrying can contribute to heightened levels of anxiety and make it difficult to manage symptoms.

Neuroticism

Neuroticism is a personality trait that is characterized by emotional instability, such as mood swings, anxiety, and irritability. People who are high in neuroticism may be more prone to developing anxiety disorders. This is because the emotional instability associated with neuroticism can contribute to heightened levels of anxiety.

Temperament

Temperament is another factor that can contribute to the development of anxiety disorders. Temperament refers to a person's innate emotional and behavioral tendencies. Some people are naturally more prone to anxiety than others. For example, children who are shy or easily overwhelmed may be more prone to developing anxiety disorders later in life.

Treatment Implications

Understanding how personality traits and temperament can contribute to the development of anxiety disorders can help inform treatment approaches. For example, cognitive-behavioral therapy (CBT) can be effective in treating anxiety disorders that are related to perfectionism or excessive worrying. CBT focuses on identifying and changing negative patterns of thought and behavior that contribute to anxiety.

Other treatment approaches for anxiety disorders may include relaxation techniques, such as deep breathing or meditation, and exposure therapy, which involves gradually exposing a person to feared situations in a safe and controlled environment.

Trauma and life experiences

Trauma and life experiences are significant factors that can contribute to the development of anxiety disorders. Below we will explore how trauma and life experiences can trigger the onset of anxiety disorders.

Trauma

Trauma is a significant factor that can contribute to the development of anxiety disorders. Trauma refers to a deeply distressing or disturbing experience, such as physical or emotional abuse, neglect, or witnessing violence.

Traumatic experiences can trigger the onset of anxiety disorders, such as post-traumatic stress disorder (PTSD).

People with PTSD may experience symptoms such as flashbacks, nightmares, and hypervigilance. They may also avoid situations or people that remind them of the traumatic event. These symptoms can significantly impact a person's daily life and make it difficult to manage their anxiety.

Life Experiences

Life experiences can also trigger the onset of anxiety disorders. Major life changes or transitions, such as moving to a new city, starting a new job, or going through a divorce, can all be stressful events that can lead to the development of anxiety disorders.

Similarly, chronic stress can also contribute to the onset of anxiety disorders. Chronic stress can come from a variety of sources, such as job stress, financial stress, or relationship stress. Over time, chronic stress can take a toll on a person's mental health and contribute to the onset of anxiety disorders.

Childhood experiences can also contribute to the development of anxiety disorders. Children who experience neglect or abuse may be more likely to develop anxiety disorders later in life. Similarly, children who grow up in an environment where they are constantly exposed to stress may be more prone to anxiety disorders.

Treatment Implications

Understanding how trauma and life experiences can contribute to the development of anxiety disorders can help inform treatment approaches. Trauma-focused therapy can be effective in treating PTSD, which is a type of anxiety disorder that can be triggered by traumatic experiences.

Cognitive-behavioral therapy (CBT) is another effective treatment approach for anxiety disorders that may be related to life experiences or chronic stress. CBT focuses on identifying and changing negative patterns of thought and behavior that contribute to anxiety. By learning new coping strategies and changing negative thought patterns, people with anxiety disorders can learn to manage their symptoms more effectively.

Other treatment approaches for anxiety disorders may include relaxation techniques, such as deep breathing or meditation, and exposure therapy, which involves gradually exposing a person to feared situations in a safe and controlled environment.

Chapter Five

Symptoms and Diagnosis

Anxiety disorders are a group of mental health conditions characterized by excessive fear, worry, and apprehension. Below we will explore the symptoms and diagnosis of anxiety disorders.

Symptoms of Anxiety Disorders

The symptoms of anxiety disorders can vary depending on the specific type of disorder a person is experiencing. However, some common symptoms of anxiety disorders include:

1. Excessive fear or worry: People with anxiety disorders may feel a sense of dread or impending doom, even when there is no apparent reason to feel that way.

2. Irritability: Anxiety disorders can also cause irritability, particularly if a person is experiencing physical symptoms, such as muscle tension or headaches.

3. Sleep disturbances: People with anxiety disorders may have difficulty falling asleep or staying asleep. They may also experience nightmares or night terrors.

4. Physical symptoms: Anxiety disorders can cause a range of physical symptoms, such as muscle tension, headaches, sweating, and nausea.

5. Avoidance: People with anxiety disorders may avoid situations or places that they fear may trigger their anxiety.

Diagnosis of Anxiety Disorders

To diagnose an anxiety disorder, a mental health professional will typically conduct a thorough assessment of a person's symptoms, medical history, and family history. They may also conduct a physical exam and run lab tests to rule out any underlying medical conditions that could be contributing to a person's symptoms.

The Diagnostic and Statistical Manual of Mental Disorders (DSM-5) is a tool commonly used by mental health professionals to diagnose mental health conditions, including anxiety disorders. The DSM-5 outlines specific diagnostic criteria for each type of anxiety disorder, which include:

6. Generalized Anxiety Disorder (GAD): To be diagnosed with GAD, a person must experience excessive worry and anxiety about a variety of different things for at least six months.

7. Panic Disorder: To be diagnosed with panic disorder, a person must experience recurring panic attacks, which are sudden episodes of intense fear or discomfort that peak within a few minutes.

8. Social Anxiety Disorder: To be diagnosed with social anxiety disorder, a person must experience intense fear or anxiety in social situations, such as speaking in public or meeting new people.

9. Specific Phobia: To be diagnosed with a specific phobia, a person must experience intense fear or anxiety in response to a specific object or situation, such as heights or spiders.

10. Separation Anxiety Disorder: To be diagnosed with separation anxiety disorder, a person must experience excessive fear or anxiety about being separated from a caregiver or loved one.

11. Agoraphobia: To be diagnosed with agoraphobia, a person must experience intense fear or anxiety in situations where escape may be difficult or help may not be available, such as crowded spaces or public transportation.

Treatment Implications

Understanding the symptoms and diagnostic criteria for anxiety disorders can help inform treatment approaches. Cognitive-behavioral therapy (CBT) is an effective treatment approach for anxiety disorders, as it focuses on identifying and changing negative patterns of thought and behavior that contribute to anxiety.

Medications, such as selective serotonin reuptake inhibitors (SSRIs), may also be used to treat anxiety disorders. SSRIs work by increasing levels of the neurotransmitter serotonin in the brain, which can help regulate mood and reduce anxiety.

Recognizing the signs of anxiety disorders

Anxiety disorders are a group of mental health conditions that can significantly impact a person's daily life. Below we will explore how to recognize the signs of anxiety disorders.

Physical Symptoms

Anxiety disorders can cause a range of physical symptoms, such as:

1. Muscle tension: People with anxiety disorders may experience muscle tension, particularly in their neck, shoulders, and back.

2. Headaches: Anxiety disorders can also cause headaches, which may be mild or severe.

3. Sweating: People with anxiety disorders may sweat excessively, even in cool or comfortable temperatures.

4. Heart palpitations: Anxiety disorders can cause heart palpitations, which may feel like a racing or pounding heart.

5. Stomach upset: Anxiety disorders can cause digestive issues, such as nausea, diarrhea, or constipation.

6. Difficulty breathing: Anxiety disorders can also make it difficult to breathe, which can cause shortness of breath or rapid breathing.

Behavioral Symptoms

Anxiety disorders can also impact a person's behavior. Some common behavioral symptoms of anxiety disorders include:

7. Avoidance: People with anxiety disorders may avoid situations or places that they fear may trigger their anxiety.

8. Procrastination: Anxiety disorders can also contribute to procrastination, particularly if a person is anxious about completing a particular task or project.

9. Irritability: Anxiety disorders can cause irritability, particularly if a person is experiencing physical symptoms, such as muscle tension or headaches.

10. Panic attacks: Panic attacks are sudden episodes of intense fear or discomfort that can cause a range of physical symptoms.

Cognitive Symptoms

Anxiety disorders can also impact a person's thoughts and cognitive processes. Some common cognitive symptoms of anxiety disorders include:

11. Excessive worry: People with anxiety disorders may worry excessively about a variety of different things, such as their health, finances, or relationships.

12. Catastrophizing: Anxiety disorders can also cause a person to catastrophize, or imagine the worst possible outcome of a situation.

13. Negative self-talk: Anxiety disorders can cause a person to engage in negative self-talk, such as criticizing themselves for perceived failures or weaknesses.

14. Difficulty concentrating: Anxiety disorders can make it difficult to concentrate or focus, particularly if a person is worried or anxious about something.

Diagnosis and Treatment

If you suspect that you or someone you know may be experiencing an anxiety disorder, it is important to seek professional help. A mental health professional can conduct a thorough assessment and provide an accurate diagnosis.

Treatment for anxiety disorders may include cognitive-behavioral therapy (CBT), medication, or a combination of both. CBT focuses on identifying and changing negative patterns of thought and behavior that contribute to anxiety. Medications, such as selective serotonin reuptake inhibitors (SSRIs), can also be effective in treating anxiety disorders.

Assessment tools and diagnostic criteria

Anxiety disorders are a group of mental health conditions characterized by excessive fear, worry, and apprehension. Below we will explore the assessment tools and diagnostic criteria used to diagnose anxiety disorders.

Assessment Tools

Assessment tools are tools used by mental health professionals to evaluate a person's symptoms and identify the presence of anxiety disorders. Some common assessment tools used to diagnose anxiety disorders include:

1. Clinical interviews: A clinical interview is a conversation between a mental health professional and a person who may be experiencing symptoms of an anxiety disorder. The mental health professional will ask questions about the person's symptoms, medical history, and family history to help determine if they have an anxiety disorder.

2. Self-report questionnaires: Self-report questionnaires are paper or online surveys that a person can complete to report their symptoms of anxiety. These questionnaires can help identify the presence and severity of anxiety symptoms.

3. Observation: Mental health professionals may also observe a person's behavior and physical symptoms to help identify the presence of anxiety disorders.

Diagnostic Criteria

The Diagnostic and Statistical Manual of Mental Disorders (DSM-5) is a tool commonly used by mental health professionals to diagnose mental health conditions, including anxiety disorders. The DSM-5 outlines specific diagnostic criteria for each type of anxiety disorder, which include:

4. Generalized Anxiety Disorder (GAD): To be diagnosed with GAD, a person must experience excessive worry and anxiety about a variety of different things for at least six months.

5. Panic Disorder: To be diagnosed with panic disorder, a person must experience recurring panic attacks, which are sudden episodes of intense fear or discomfort that peak within a few minutes.

6. Social Anxiety Disorder: To be diagnosed with social anxiety disorder, a person must experience intense fear or anxiety in social situations, such as speaking in public or meeting new people.

7. Specific Phobia: To be diagnosed with a specific phobia, a person must experience intense fear or anxiety in response to a specific object or situation, such as heights or spiders.

8. Separation Anxiety Disorder: To be diagnosed with separation anxiety disorder, a person must experience excessive fear or anxiety about being separated from a caregiver or loved one.

9. Agoraphobia: To be diagnosed with agoraphobia, a person must experience intense fear or anxiety in situations where escape may be difficult or help may not be available, such as crowded spaces or public transportation.

Treatment Implications

Understanding the assessment tools and diagnostic criteria for anxiety disorders can help inform treatment approaches. Cognitive-behavioral therapy (CBT) is an effective treatment approach for anxiety disorders, as it focuses on identifying and changing negative patterns of thought and behavior that contribute to anxiety.

Medications, such as selective serotonin reuptake inhibitors (SSRIs), may also be used to treat anxiety disorders. SSRIs work by increasing levels of the neurotransmitter serotonin in the brain, which can help regulate mood and reduce anxiety.

The importance of early intervention

Anxiety disorders are a group of mental health conditions that can significantly impact a person's daily life. Early intervention is essential in managing anxiety disorders and preventing them from worsening. Below we will explore the importance of early intervention for anxiety disorders.

Identifying Anxiety Disorders Early

The first step in early intervention for anxiety disorders is identifying them early. Unfortunately, many people with anxiety disorders go undiagnosed or do not seek treatment for their symptoms. This can lead to a range of negative consequences, including increased severity of symptoms and decreased quality of life.

There are several signs and symptoms of anxiety disorders that can be identified early, including:

Excessive worry or fear about specific situations or events

Difficulty sleeping or staying asleep

Physical symptoms such as sweating, shaking, or nausea

Avoidance of situations or activities that may trigger anxiety

Difficulty concentrating or focusing

If you or someone you know is experiencing these symptoms, it is important to seek professional help as soon as possible.

The Importance of Early Intervention

Early intervention for anxiety disorders can have several benefits, including:

1. Improved Outcomes: The earlier an anxiety disorder is identified and treated, the more likely it is that a person will experience improved outcomes. Treatment approaches such as cognitive-behavioral therapy (CBT) can be highly effective in managing anxiety disorders when implemented early.

2. Preventing Worsening Symptoms: Without treatment, anxiety disorders can worsen over time, leading to more severe symptoms and a decreased quality of life. Early intervention can help prevent this from happening.

3. Improved Daily Functioning: Anxiety disorders can significantly impact a person's daily life, making it difficult to perform everyday tasks such as going to work or school. Early intervention can help improve a person's daily functioning and overall quality of life.

4. Reduced Risk of Comorbidities: Anxiety disorders are often comorbid with other mental health conditions such as depression. Early intervention can help reduce the risk of these comorbidities developing.

Treatment Approaches for Anxiety Disorders

There are several treatment approaches that can be effective in managing anxiety disorders when implemented early. These include:

5. Cognitive-Behavioral Therapy (CBT): CBT is a type of therapy that focuses on identifying and changing negative patterns of thought and behavior that contribute to anxiety. CBT has been shown to be highly effective in managing anxiety disorders.

6. Medication: Medications such as selective serotonin reuptake inhibitors (SSRIs) can be effective in managing anxiety disorders. Medications can be particularly helpful for people with severe symptoms or those who do not respond to other treatment approaches.

7. Lifestyle Changes: Making lifestyle changes such as getting regular exercise, practicing relaxation techniques, and avoiding substances such as caffeine and alcohol can also be helpful in managing anxiety disorders.

Chapter Six

Comorbid Conditions

Anxiety disorders are a group of mental health conditions characterized by excessive fear, worry, and apprehension. These disorders are often comorbid with other mental health conditions, which can complicate treatment and management. Below we will explore the comorbid conditions commonly associated with anxiety disorders.

Depression

Depression is one of the most common comorbidities associated with anxiety disorders. The symptoms of depression, such as feelings of sadness, hopelessness, and loss of interest in activities, can overlap with symptoms of anxiety disorders, making it difficult to differentiate between the two conditions.

Substance Use Disorders

Substance use disorders are also commonly comorbid with anxiety disorders. People with anxiety disorders may turn to drugs or alcohol as a way to cope with their symptoms. Unfortunately, substance use can exacerbate anxiety symptoms and lead to a range of negative consequences, including addiction and physical health problems.

Eating Disorders

Eating disorders, such as anorexia nervosa and bulimia nervosa, are also commonly comorbid with anxiety disorders. These conditions often co-occur due to the shared underlying psychological and biological factors, such as low self-esteem and genetics.

Obsessive-Compulsive Disorder (OCD)

Obsessive-compulsive disorder (OCD) is another condition commonly associated with anxiety disorders. OCD is characterized by intrusive, unwanted thoughts or impulses, often followed by repetitive behaviors or rituals. People with anxiety disorders may experience obsessive thoughts or compulsions related to their fears or worries.

Post-Traumatic Stress Disorder (PTSD)

Post-traumatic stress disorder (PTSD) is a mental health condition that can develop after a person experiences or witnesses a traumatic event. People with anxiety disorders may have a higher risk of developing PTSD, as they may be more sensitive to stress and trauma.

Borderline Personality Disorder (BPD)

Borderline personality disorder (BPD) is a mental health condition characterized by unstable moods, behaviors, and relationships. BPD often co-occurs with anxiety disorders, as both conditions share underlying emotional dysregulation and impulsivity.

Attention-Deficit/Hyperactivity Disorder (ADHD)

Attention-deficit/hyperactivity disorder (ADHD) is a neurodevelopmental disorder characterized by inattention, hyperactivity, and impulsivity. People with anxiety disorders may have a higher risk of developing ADHD, as anxiety can interfere with attention and concentration.

Treatment Implications

The comorbidity of anxiety disorders with other mental health conditions can complicate treatment and management. Treatment approaches may need to address multiple conditions simultaneously. Cognitive-behavioral therapy (CBT) is an effective treatment approach for anxiety disorders and some of their comorbidities, such as depression and PTSD. Medications, such as antidepressants and antipsychotics, may also be used to treat co-morbid conditions.

Depression and mood disorders

Depression and anxiety are two of the most common mental health conditions, and they often co-occur. Below we will explore the relationship between anxiety disorders and depression, as well as other mood disorders.

Depression and Anxiety

Depression and anxiety disorders often co-occur, and the symptoms of each condition can exacerbate the other. For example, feelings of sadness and hopelessness associated with depression can lead to increased anxiety, while excessive worry and fear associated with anxiety can contribute to feelings of depression.

Some common symptoms of depression include:

Persistent feelings of sadness or hopelessness

Loss of interest in activities

Changes in appetite or weight

Sleep disturbances

Fatigue or low energy

Difficulty concentrating or making decisions

Thoughts of death or suicide

Some common symptoms of anxiety disorders include:

Excessive worry or fear about specific situations or events

Avoidance of situations or activities that may trigger anxiety

Physical symptoms such as sweating, shaking, or nausea

Difficulty sleeping or staying asleep

Difficulty concentrating or focusing

Mood Disorders

Mood disorders are a group of mental health conditions characterized by disturbances in mood, such as depression or mania. In addition to depression, several other mood disorders can co-occur with anxiety disorders:

Bipolar Disorder

Bipolar disorder is a mood disorder characterized by alternating periods of depression and mania. Mania is a state of heightened energy and excitement, often accompanied by irritability, impulsivity, and a decreased need for sleep.

Cyclothymic Disorder

Cyclothymic disorder is a milder form of bipolar disorder characterized by alternating periods of hypomania (a milder form of mania) and depression.

Persistent Depressive Disorder

Persistent depressive disorder, also known as dysthymia, is a chronic form of depression characterized by persistent feelings of sadness or hopelessness for at least two years.

Treatment Approaches

The co-occurrence of anxiety disorders and mood disorders can complicate treatment and management. Treatment approaches may need to address both conditions simultaneously. Some treatment approaches for anxiety disorders and mood disorders include:

Cognitive-Behavioral Therapy (CBT)

CBT is a type of therapy that focuses on identifying and changing negative patterns of thought and behavior that contribute to anxiety and depression. CBT can be effective in managing both conditions when implemented early.

Medication

Medications such as selective serotonin reuptake inhibitors (SSRIs) can be effective in managing both anxiety and depression. Medications can be particularly helpful for people with severe symptoms or those who do not respond to other treatment approaches.

Lifestyle Changes

Making lifestyle changes such as getting regular exercise, practicing relaxation techniques, and avoiding substances such as caffeine and alcohol can also be helpful in managing both anxiety and depression.

Obsessive-Compulsive Disorder (OCD)

Obsessive-Compulsive Disorder (OCD) is a type of anxiety disorder characterized by intrusive, unwanted thoughts or impulses, often followed by repetitive behaviors or rituals. OCD affects approximately 1-2% of the population worldwide, making it a relatively common mental health condition. Below we will explore the symptoms, causes, and treatment options for OCD.

Symptoms

The symptoms of OCD can vary from person to person, but typically involve obsessions and compulsions. Obsessions are unwanted, intrusive thoughts or impulses that cause significant distress, while compulsions are repetitive behaviors or mental acts that are performed in response to obsessions. Some common obsessions and compulsions associated with OCD include:

Obsessions:

Fear of contamination or germs

Intrusive violent or sexual thoughts

Fear of causing harm or being responsible for a negative event

Excessive concern with order, symmetry, or exactness

Compulsions:

Excessive washing or cleaning

Repeating certain words, phrases, or prayers

Counting or arranging objects in a specific way

Checking and rechecking to make sure something is done correctly or to prevent harm

Causes

The exact cause of OCD is unknown, but research suggests that a combination of genetic, environmental, and neurological factors may play a role. Some possible risk factors for OCD include:

1. Genetics: OCD tends to run in families, suggesting a genetic component.

2. Brain abnormalities: Differences in brain structure and function have been observed in people with OCD.

3. Environmental factors: Trauma, abuse, and chronic stress may increase the risk of developing OCD.

4. Neurotransmitter imbalances: OCD may be related to imbalances in neurotransmitters such as serotonin, dopamine, and glutamate.

Treatment

OCD can be a challenging condition to treat, but several effective treatment options are available. Treatment typically involves a combination of medication, therapy, and lifestyle changes. Some common treatment options for OCD include:

Cognitive-Behavioral Therapy (CBT)

CBT is a type of therapy that focuses on identifying and changing negative patterns of thought and behavior that contribute to OCD. Exposure and response prevention (ERP) is a specific type of CBT that involves gradually exposing the person to feared objects or situations and teaching them strategies to resist compulsions.

Medication

Medications such as selective serotonin reuptake inhibitors (SSRIs) and tricyclic antidepressants can be effective in managing symptoms of OCD.

These medications work by increasing levels of serotonin, a neurotransmitter that is involved in mood regulation.

Lifestyle Changes

Making lifestyle changes such as getting regular exercise, practicing relaxation techniques, and avoiding substances such as caffeine and alcohol can also be helpful in managing OCD symptoms.

Post-Traumatic Stress Disorder (PTSD)

Post-Traumatic Stress Disorder (PTSD) is a mental health condition that can develop after a person experiences or witnesses a traumatic event. PTSD is a type of anxiety disorder that affects approximately 7-8% of the population in their lifetime. Below we will explore the symptoms, causes, and treatment options for PTSD.

Symptoms

The symptoms of PTSD can vary from person to person, but typically fall into four categories: re-experiencing, avoidance, hyperarousal, and negative changes in mood and cognition. Some common symptoms of PTSD include:

Re-Experiencing:

Flashbacks or intrusive memories of the traumatic event

Nightmares related to the traumatic event

Physical or emotional reactions to reminders of the event

Avoidance:

Avoidance of people, places, or situations that remind the person of the traumatic event

Loss of interest in activities that the person used to enjoy

Emotional numbing or detachment

Hyperarousal:

Hypervigilance or being constantly on guard

Irritability or outbursts of anger

Difficulty concentrating or sleeping

Negative Changes in Mood and Cognition:

Persistent negative beliefs or feelings about oneself or others

Feeling detached or estranged from others

Difficulty experiencing positive emotions

Causes

PTSD can develop after a person experiences or witnesses a traumatic event, such as military combat, sexual assault, or a natural disaster. While not everyone who experiences a traumatic event will develop PTSD, some risk factors may increase the likelihood of developing the disorder, such as:

A history of trauma or abuse

A family history of mental health conditions

Pre-existing anxiety or depression

Lack of social support after the traumatic event

Treatment

PTSD can be a challenging condition to treat, but several effective treatment options are available. Treatment typically involves a combination of medication, therapy, and lifestyle changes. Some common treatment options for PTSD include:

Cognitive-Behavioral Therapy (CBT)

CBT is a type of therapy that focuses on identifying and changing negative patterns of thought and behavior that contribute to PTSD. Exposure therapy, a specific type of CBT, involves gradually exposing the person to reminders of the traumatic event and teaching them strategies to manage their emotional reactions.

Medication

Medications such as selective serotonin reuptake inhibitors (SSRIs) and prazosin can be effective in managing symptoms of PTSD. SSRIs work by increasing levels of serotonin, a neurotransmitter that is involved in mood regulation, while prazosin is used to manage nightmares and sleep disturbances.

Lifestyle Changes

Making lifestyle changes such as getting regular exercise, practicing relaxation techniques, and avoiding substances such as caffeine and alcohol can also be helpful in managing PTSD symptoms.

Eating disorders

Eating disorders are a group of mental health conditions characterized by disturbed eating behaviors and a preoccupation with body weight or shape. Eating disorders affect both men and women and typically develop during adolescence or early adulthood. Below we will explore the symptoms, causes, and treatment options for eating disorders.

Symptoms

The symptoms of eating disorders can vary from person to person, but typically involve a preoccupation with food and weight. Some common symptoms of eating disorders include:

Anorexia Nervosa:

Refusal to maintain a healthy body weight

Intense fear of gaining weight

Distorted body image

Amenorrhea in women

Bulimia Nervosa:

Recurrent episodes of binge eating followed by purging behaviors (such as vomiting, laxative use, or excessive exercise)

Preoccupation with body weight and shape

Feeling out of control during binge episodes

Shame or guilt after bingeing and purging

Binge Eating Disorder:

Recurrent episodes of binge eating (eating large amounts of food in a short amount of time)

Feeling out of control during binge episodes

Eating until uncomfortably full or experiencing physical discomfort from the amount of food consumed

Feeling guilty or ashamed after binge eating episodes

Causes

The exact cause of eating disorders is unknown, but a combination of genetic, environmental, and psychological factors may play a role. Some possible risk factors for eating disorders include:

1. Genetics: Eating disorders tend to run in families, suggesting a genetic component.

2. Environmental factors: Cultural pressure to be thin, peer pressure, and stress may contribute to the development of eating disorders.

3. Psychological factors: Eating disorders may be related to anxiety, depression, or low self-esteem.

4. Neurotransmitter imbalances: Eating disorders may be related to imbalances in neurotransmitters such as serotonin, dopamine, and norepinephrine.

Treatment

Eating disorders can be a challenging condition to treat, but several effective treatment options are available. Treatment typically involves a combination of medication, therapy, and lifestyle changes. Some common treatment options for eating disorders include:

Cognitive-Behavioral Therapy (CBT)

CBT is a type of therapy that focuses on identifying and changing negative patterns of thought and behavior that contribute to eating disorders. It may involve challenging unrealistic beliefs about body weight and shape and teaching strategies to manage disordered eating behaviors.

Medication

Medications such as antidepressants may be used in combination with therapy to manage symptoms of eating disorders. These medications can help to regulate mood and reduce symptoms of anxiety or depression that may contribute to disordered eating behaviors.

Nutritional Counseling

Working with a registered dietitian can be helpful in managing eating disorders. Nutritional counseling can involve developing healthy eating habits, learning how to read food labels, and developing a positive relationship with food.

Substance use disorders

Substance use disorders are a group of mental health conditions characterized by a problematic pattern of substance use that leads to significant impairment or distress. Substance use disorders can affect individuals of any age, gender, or background, and can have serious consequences for physical and mental health. Below we will explore the symptoms, causes, and treatment options for substance use disorders.

Symptoms

The symptoms of substance use disorders can vary depending on the substance being used, but typically involve a problematic pattern of use that leads to significant impairment or distress. Some common symptoms of substance use disorders include:

Using the substance in larger amounts or for longer periods than intended

Being unable to cut down or stop using the substance despite wanting to do so

Spending a significant amount of time obtaining or using the substance

Craving the substance when not using it

Continuing to use the substance despite negative consequences such as health problems, relationship issues, or legal troubles

Causes

The exact cause of substance use disorders is unknown, but a combination of genetic, environmental, and psychological factors may play a role. Some possible risk factors for substance use disorders include:

1. Genetics: Substance use disorders tend to run in families, suggesting a genetic component.

2. Environmental factors: Exposure to trauma, stress, or peer pressure may contribute to the development of substance use disorders.

3. Psychological factors: Substance use disorders may be related to anxiety, depression, or other mental health conditions.

4. Social factors: Social isolation, lack of social support, or lack of access to resources may contribute to the development of substance use disorders.

Treatment

Substance use disorders can be a challenging condition to treat, but several effective treatment options are available. Treatment typically involves a combination of medication, therapy, and lifestyle changes. Some common treatment options for substance use disorders include:

Medication

Medications such as methadone, buprenorphine, and naltrexone can be used to manage withdrawal symptoms and cravings associated with substance use disorders. Medications such as disulfiram and acamprosate can also be used to manage alcohol dependence.

Behavioral Therapy

Behavioral therapy, such as cognitive-behavioral therapy (CBT) and motivational interviewing, can help individuals with substance use disorders identify and change negative patterns of thought and behavior that contribute to substance use.

Support Groups

Support groups, such as Alcoholics Anonymous (AA) or Narcotics Anonymous (NA), can provide individuals with substance use disorders with a sense of community and support as they work to overcome their addiction.

Chapter Seven

Treatment Options

Anxiety disorders can be a challenging condition to live with, but effective treatment options are available to help individuals manage their symptoms and improve their quality of life. Treatment typically involves a combination of medication, therapy, and lifestyle changes. Below we will explore the different treatment options available for anxiety disorders.

Medication

Medication can be an effective treatment option for managing symptoms of anxiety disorders. Several different types of medications are used to treat anxiety disorders, including:

1. Antidepressants: Antidepressants, such as selective serotonin reuptake inhibitors (SSRIs) and serotonin-norepinephrine reuptake inhibitors (SNRIs), can be used to manage symptoms of anxiety disorders. These medications work by increasing the levels of neurotransmitters in the brain that are associated with mood and anxiety regulation.

2. Benzodiazepines: Benzodiazepines, such as diazepam and alprazolam, are a class of medications that can be used to manage acute anxiety symptoms. However, they can be addictive and have the potential for abuse, so they are typically used only for short periods of time.

3. Beta-blockers: Beta-blockers, such as propranolol, can be used to manage physical symptoms of anxiety, such as rapid heartbeat and sweating.

It is important to note that medications should be prescribed and monitored by a healthcare professional.

Therapy

Several different types of therapy can be used to manage symptoms of anxiety disorders. These therapies include:

4. Cognitive-Behavioral Therapy (CBT): CBT is a type of therapy that focuses on identifying and changing negative patterns of thought and behavior that contribute to anxiety. It may involve challenging unrealistic beliefs about anxiety and teaching strategies to manage anxiety symptoms.

5. Exposure Therapy: Exposure therapy involves gradually exposing individuals to feared situations or objects in a safe and controlled environment. This can help individuals learn to manage their anxiety symptoms and reduce their fear response.

6. Acceptance and Commitment Therapy (ACT): ACT is a type of therapy that focuses on accepting uncomfortable thoughts and feelings rather than trying to avoid them. It may involve mindfulness techniques and developing a sense of purpose or meaning in life.

Lifestyle Changes

Lifestyle changes can also be an effective way to manage symptoms of anxiety disorders. These changes include:

7. Exercise: Regular exercise can help reduce symptoms of anxiety and improve overall physical and mental health.

8. Relaxation Techniques: Relaxation techniques, such as deep breathing, progressive muscle relaxation, and meditation, can help manage anxiety symptoms and reduce stress.

9. Healthy Eating Habits: Eating a balanced diet and avoiding caffeine and alcohol can help manage anxiety symptoms.

Cognitive-Behavioral Therapy (CBT)

Cognitive-behavioral therapy (CBT) is a type of psychotherapy that is commonly used to treat anxiety disorders. CBT focuses on identifying and changing negative patterns of thought and behavior that contribute to anxiety. Below we will explore the principles and techniques of CBT and its effectiveness in treating anxiety disorders.

Principles of CBT

CBT is based on the idea that our thoughts, feelings, and behaviors are interconnected and can influence one another. Negative thoughts and beliefs can lead to negative feelings and behaviors, which can perpetuate the cycle of anxiety. CBT aims to help individuals identify and challenge these negative thoughts and beliefs in order to change their behavior and improve their mental health.

Techniques of CBT

CBT uses several different techniques to help individuals manage anxiety symptoms. Some of these techniques include:

1. Identifying Negative Thoughts: CBT begins by identifying negative thoughts and beliefs that contribute to anxiety. This may involve keeping a journal of negative thoughts or beliefs and challenging them using evidence and logic.

2. Relaxation Techniques: CBT may involve teaching relaxation techniques such as deep breathing, progressive muscle relaxation, and mindfulness to help manage anxiety symptoms.

3. Exposure Therapy: Exposure therapy involves gradually exposing individuals to feared situations or objects in a safe and controlled environment. This can help individuals learn to manage their anxiety symptoms and reduce their fear response.

4. Cognitive Restructuring: Cognitive restructuring involves identifying and challenging negative thoughts and beliefs that contribute to anxiety. This may involve using evidence and logic to challenge unrealistic beliefs about anxiety.

5. Behavioral Activation: Behavioral activation involves identifying and participating in positive activities that can improve mood and reduce anxiety. This may involve developing a plan to engage in enjoyable and meaningful activities.

Effectiveness of CBT

CBT has been shown to be an effective treatment for anxiety disorders. Research studies have found that CBT is as effective as medication in treating anxiety disorders and may have longer-lasting effects. CBT has been found to be effective in treating a range of anxiety disorders, including generalized anxiety disorder, social anxiety disorder, and panic disorder.

CBT can also be effective in preventing relapse of anxiety symptoms. In one study, individuals who received CBT for social anxiety disorder were less likely to relapse than those who received medication.

Exposure Therapy

Exposure therapy is a type of behavioral therapy that is commonly used to treat anxiety disorders. The goal of exposure therapy is to gradually expose individuals to feared situations or objects in a safe and controlled environment, with the aim of reducing anxiety and fear responses. Below we will explore the principles and techniques of exposure therapy and its effectiveness in treating anxiety disorders.

Principles of Exposure Therapy

Exposure therapy is based on the principles of classical conditioning. Classical conditioning is a type of learning in which a neutral stimulus becomes associated with a previously learned response. For example, a person may develop a fear of dogs after being bitten by a dog. In this case, the dog becomes associated with the fear response.

Exposure therapy aims to break the association between the feared stimulus and the fear response. By gradually exposing individuals to the feared stimulus in a safe and controlled environment, individuals can learn that the feared stimulus is not as dangerous as they previously believed. Over time, this can lead to a reduction in anxiety and fear responses.

Techniques of Exposure Therapy

Exposure therapy uses several different techniques to help individuals manage anxiety symptoms. Some of these techniques include:

1. Systematic Desensitization: Systematic desensitization involves gradually exposing individuals to feared situations or objects while teaching relaxation techniques to manage anxiety symptoms. This can help individuals learn to manage their anxiety symptoms and reduce their fear response.

2. Flooding: Flooding involves exposing individuals to the most feared situation or object without the use of relaxation techniques. This can be an effective technique for individuals with specific phobias, but may not be appropriate for individuals with more severe anxiety disorders.

3. Virtual Reality Therapy: Virtual reality therapy involves using virtual reality technology to simulate feared situations or objects in a safe and controlled environment. This can be an effective technique for individuals who are unable to participate in in vivo exposure therapy.

Effectiveness of Exposure Therapy

Exposure therapy has been shown to be an effective treatment for anxiety disorders. Research studies have found that exposure therapy is as effective as medication in treating anxiety disorders and may have longer-lasting effects. Exposure therapy has been found to be effective in treating a range of anxiety disorders, including generalized anxiety disorder, social anxiety disorder, and specific phobias.

Exposure therapy can also be effective in preventing relapse of anxiety symptoms. In one study, individuals who received exposure therapy for specific phobias were less likely to relapse than those who received medication.

Acceptance and Commitment Therapy (ACT)

Acceptance and Commitment Therapy (ACT) is a type of psychotherapy that is commonly used to treat anxiety disorders. ACT aims to help individuals accept their thoughts and emotions rather than trying to control or avoid them. Below we will explore the principles and techniques of ACT and its effectiveness in treating anxiety disorders.

Principles of ACT

ACT is based on the idea that attempts to control or avoid negative thoughts and emotions can actually increase anxiety and distress. Instead of trying to control or avoid these thoughts and emotions, ACT encourages individuals to accept them as a normal part of the human experience. ACT also emphasizes the importance of living a meaningful and values-driven life, even in the presence of difficult thoughts and emotions.

Techniques of ACT

ACT uses several different techniques to help individuals manage anxiety symptoms. Some of these techniques include:

1. Mindfulness: Mindfulness involves paying attention to the present moment in a non-judgmental way. This can help individuals learn to accept their thoughts and emotions without trying to control or avoid them.

2. Values Clarification: Values clarification involves identifying and clarifying personal values and goals. This can help individuals identify what is most important to them and make decisions based on these values, even in the presence of difficult thoughts and emotions.

3. Cognitive Defusion: Cognitive defusion involves learning to view thoughts as just thoughts, rather than as accurate reflections of reality. This can help individuals learn to accept their thoughts without becoming overwhelmed by them.

4. Committed Action: Committed action involves taking steps towards living a meaningful and values-driven life, even in the presence of difficult thoughts and emotions.

Effectiveness of ACT

ACT has been shown to be an effective treatment for anxiety disorders. Research studies have found that ACT is as effective as traditional cognitive-behavioral therapy in treating anxiety disorders and may have longer-lasting effects. ACT has been found to be effective in treating a range of anxiety disorders, including generalized anxiety disorder, social anxiety disorder, and panic disorder.

ACT can also be effective in preventing relapse of anxiety symptoms. In one study, individuals who received ACT for social anxiety disorder were less likely to relapse than those who received traditional cognitive-behavioral therapy.

Dialectical Behavior Therapy (DBT)

Dialectical Behavior Therapy (DBT) is a type of psychotherapy that was initially developed to treat individuals with borderline personality disorder. However, it has since been adapted to treat a variety of mental health conditions, including anxiety disorders. Below we will explore the principles and techniques of DBT and its effectiveness in treating anxiety disorders.

Principles of DBT

DBT is based on the idea that individuals may have difficulty regulating their emotions and coping with distressing situations. The therapy aims to help individuals build skills to manage difficult emotions and improve relationships with others. DBT is often delivered in a group setting, but individual therapy sessions may also be included.

Techniques of DBT

DBT uses a variety of techniques to help individuals manage anxiety symptoms. Some of these techniques include:

1. Mindfulness: Mindfulness involves paying attention to the present moment in a non-judgmental way. This can help individuals learn to accept their thoughts and emotions without trying to control or avoid them.

2. Distress Tolerance: Distress tolerance skills help individuals tolerate difficult emotions and situations without resorting to harmful behaviors.

These skills include distraction techniques, self-soothing techniques, and improving the moment.

3. Emotion Regulation: Emotion regulation skills help individuals identify and manage intense emotions. These skills include identifying emotions, reducing emotional vulnerability, increasing positive emotions, and decreasing negative emotions.

4. Interpersonal Effectiveness: Interpersonal effectiveness skills help individuals build and maintain positive relationships with others. These skills include effective communication, assertiveness, and setting healthy boundaries.

Effectiveness of DBT

DBT has been found to be effective in treating a variety of mental health conditions, including anxiety disorders. Research studies have found that DBT can be effective in reducing symptoms of generalized anxiety disorder, social anxiety disorder, and post-traumatic stress disorder.

DBT has also been found to be effective in reducing self-harm and suicidal behaviors in individuals with borderline personality disorder. In addition, DBT has been found to be effective in improving overall functioning and quality of life in individuals with anxiety disorders.

Medications

Anxiety disorders are a group of mental health conditions that can cause significant distress and impairment in daily life. While therapy is often the first line of treatment for anxiety disorders, medications can also be a useful tool in managing symptoms. Below we will explore the different types of medications used to treat anxiety disorders, their mechanisms of action, and their potential side effects.

Types of Medications

Selective Serotonin Reuptake Inhibitors (SSRIs)

SSRIs are a type of antidepressant that are commonly used to treat anxiety disorders. They work by increasing the amount of serotonin in the brain, which can improve mood and reduce anxiety symptoms. Examples of SSRIs include fluoxetine (Prozac), sertraline (Zoloft), and escitalopram (Lexapro).

Serotonin-Norepinephrine Reuptake Inhibitors (SNRIs)

SNRIs are another type of antidepressant that are sometimes used to treat anxiety disorders. They work by increasing the levels of both serotonin and norepinephrine in the brain, which can improve mood and reduce anxiety symptoms. Examples of SNRIs include venlafaxine (Effexor) and duloxetine (Cymbalta).

Benzodiazepines

Benzodiazepines are a type of sedative medication that are sometimes used to treat anxiety disorders. They work by enhancing the effects of a neurotransmitter called gamma-aminobutyric acid (GABA), which can reduce anxiety and promote relaxation. Examples of benzodiazepines include alprazolam (Xanax), lorazepam (Ativan), and diazepam (Valium).

Beta-Blockers

Beta-blockers are a type of medication that are sometimes used to treat the physical symptoms of anxiety, such as rapid heart rate, trembling, and sweating. They work by blocking the effects of adrenaline on the body, which can reduce physical symptoms of anxiety. Examples of beta-blockers include propranolol (Inderal) and atenolol (Tenormin).

Mechanisms of Action

Each type of medication used to treat anxiety disorders works in a different way. SSRIs and SNRIs increase the levels of certain neurotransmitters in the brain, which can improve mood and reduce anxiety symptoms. Benzodiazepines enhance the effects of GABA, which can promote relaxation and reduce anxiety. Beta-blockers block the effects of adrenaline on the body, which can reduce physical symptoms of anxiety.

Potential Side Effects

While medications can be useful in managing anxiety symptoms, they can also have potential side effects. Some of the potential side effects of medications used to treat anxiety disorders include:

1. SSRIs and SNRIs: nausea, headache, insomnia, sexual dysfunction, and increased risk of suicide in young adults.

2. Benzodiazepines: drowsiness, dizziness, confusion, memory problems, and risk of dependence or addiction.

3. Beta-blockers: fatigue, dizziness, and low blood pressure.

It is important to discuss potential side effects with your healthcare provider before starting any medication.

Chapter Eight

Alternative and Complementary Treatments

Anxiety disorders are a group of mental health conditions that can cause significant distress and impairment in daily life. While traditional treatments such as therapy and medication are often effective, some people may also turn to alternative and complementary treatments to manage their anxiety symptoms. Below we will explore some of the alternative and complementary treatments that may be used to treat anxiety disorders, their mechanisms of action, and their potential benefits and risks.

Mindfulness Meditation

Mindfulness meditation is a form of meditation that involves focusing on the present moment and accepting one's thoughts and feelings without judgment. This practice has been shown to be effective in reducing symptoms of anxiety, depression, and stress. It may work by helping people to become more aware of their thoughts and emotions and to develop a greater sense of control over them.

Yoga

Yoga is a form of exercise that combines physical postures with breathing techniques and meditation. It has been shown to be effective in reducing symptoms of anxiety, depression, and stress. Yoga may work by promoting relaxation and reducing tension in the body, as well as improving mood and increasing feelings of well-being.

Acupuncture

Acupuncture is a form of traditional Chinese medicine that involves the insertion of thin needles into specific points on the body. It has been shown to be effective in reducing symptoms of anxiety, and may work by regulating the flow of energy in the body and promoting relaxation.

Herbal Supplements

There are several herbal supplements that may be used to treat anxiety, such as kava, valerian root, and passionflower. These supplements may work by increasing levels of certain neurotransmitters in the brain, such as gamma-aminobutyric acid (GABA), which can promote relaxation and reduce anxiety symptoms. However, it is important to use caution when using herbal supplements, as they can interact with other medications and may have potential side effects.

Massage Therapy

Massage therapy involves the manipulation of soft tissues in the body to promote relaxation and reduce tension. It has been shown to be effective in reducing symptoms of anxiety, and may work by promoting relaxation and reducing muscle tension.

Aromatherapy

Aromatherapy involves the use of essential oils to promote relaxation and reduce anxiety symptoms. Oils such as lavender, chamomile, and bergamot may be used to promote relaxation and reduce anxiety. Aromatherapy may work by activating certain areas of the brain that are involved in mood and emotion regulation.

Potential Benefits and Risks

Alternative and complementary treatments for anxiety disorders may offer several potential benefits, such as reducing symptoms of anxiety, promoting relaxation, and improving overall well-being. However, it is important to note that these treatments may not work for everyone and may have potential risks and side effects.

For example, while mindfulness meditation and yoga are generally considered safe, some people may experience discomfort or injury if they are not practiced properly. Acupuncture may also carry a risk of infection or injury if not performed by a qualified practitioner. Herbal supplements may interact with other medications and may have potential side effects, such as dizziness, drowsiness, or upset stomach. Massage therapy and aromatherapy may be safe for most people, but some individuals may experience discomfort or adverse reactions.

It is important to discuss any alternative or complementary treatments with your healthcare provider before trying them, especially if you are currently taking medication or have a pre-existing medical condition.

Mindfulness and meditation

Mindfulness and meditation have become increasingly popular as techniques to manage mental health conditions such as anxiety disorders. Below we will explore what mindfulness and meditation are, how they can benefit those with anxiety disorders, and some of the different techniques that can be used.

What is Mindfulness?

Mindfulness is the practice of paying attention to the present moment without judgment. This means observing one's thoughts, feelings, and surroundings without getting caught up in them or reacting to them. It involves being fully present in the moment and accepting things as they are, rather than trying to change or control them.

What is Meditation?

Meditation is a practice that involves training the mind to focus on a specific object or thought, such as the breath, a mantra, or a visualization. This can help to cultivate a sense of calmness and relaxation, as well as increase awareness and concentration. There are many different types of meditation, but they all involve some form of focus and attention training.

How can Mindfulness and Meditation Benefit Those with Anxiety Disorders?

Anxiety disorders are characterized by persistent feelings of worry, fear, and apprehension that can interfere with daily life. Mindfulness and meditation can be effective tools for managing these symptoms and promoting overall well-being.

Reduce Anxiety Symptoms

One of the primary benefits of mindfulness and meditation is their ability to reduce symptoms of anxiety. By focusing on the present moment and accepting one's thoughts and feelings without judgment, individuals can learn to manage anxious thoughts and feelings more effectively.

Improve Mood

Mindfulness and meditation have also been shown to improve mood and reduce symptoms of depression. These practices can help individuals to develop a greater sense of well-being and overall satisfaction with their lives.

Increase Resilience

Mindfulness and meditation can also increase resilience, or the ability to bounce back from adversity. By learning to observe their thoughts and feelings without judgment, individuals can develop a greater sense of control over their emotions and become better equipped to handle stress and challenges.

Improve Sleep

Anxiety disorders can often interfere with sleep, but mindfulness and meditation can help to promote relaxation and improve sleep quality. By focusing on the present moment and cultivating a sense of calmness, individuals may be better able to fall asleep and stay asleep throughout the night.

Different Techniques for Mindfulness and Meditation

Mindfulness-Based Stress Reduction (MBSR)

MBSR is a program developed by Dr. Jon Kabat-Zinn that combines mindfulness meditation with yoga and other mind-body techniques. This program has been shown to be effective in reducing symptoms of anxiety and depression and improving overall well-being.

Loving-Kindness Meditation

Loving-kindness meditation involves cultivating feelings of love, kindness, and compassion towards oneself and others. This technique can help to reduce negative emotions such as anger and resentment and promote feelings of connection and empathy.

Body Scan Meditation

Body scan meditation involves focusing on different parts of the body and observing any sensations that arise. This technique can help individuals to become more aware of their physical sensations and develop a greater sense of connection to their bodies.

Breathing Meditation

Breathing meditation involves focusing on the breath and observing any thoughts or distractions that arise. This technique can help to promote relaxation and reduce symptoms of anxiety.

Yoga and relaxation techniques

Yoga and relaxation techniques are popular practices used to manage anxiety disorders. Below we will explore what yoga and relaxation techniques are, how they can benefit those with anxiety disorders, and some of the different techniques that can be used.

What is Yoga?

Yoga is an ancient practice that combines physical postures, breathing exercises, and meditation techniques to promote physical and mental well-being. There are many different styles of yoga, each with its own focus and approach, but all share a common goal of promoting mindfulness and relaxation.

How can Yoga Benefit Those with Anxiety Disorders?

Yoga has been shown to have a number of benefits for those with anxiety disorders, including:

Reduce Anxiety Symptoms

Yoga can help to reduce symptoms of anxiety by promoting relaxation and reducing stress. By focusing on breathing and physical movement, individuals can learn to manage anxious thoughts and feelings more effectively.

Improve Mood

Yoga has also been shown to improve mood and reduce symptoms of depression. These practices can help individuals to develop a greater sense of well-being and overall satisfaction with their lives.

Increase Resilience

Yoga can help to increase resilience, or the ability to bounce back from adversity. By learning to observe their thoughts and feelings without judgment, individuals can develop a greater sense of control over their emotions and become better equipped to handle stress and challenges.

Improve Sleep

Yoga can also help to improve sleep quality, which can be particularly beneficial for those with anxiety disorders. By promoting relaxation and reducing stress, individuals may be better able to fall asleep and stay asleep throughout the night.

Different Types of Yoga and Relaxation Techniques

Hatha Yoga

Hatha yoga is a gentle form of yoga that focuses on breathing and basic yoga poses. This style is particularly well-suited for beginners and those looking for a more gentle practice.

Vinyasa Yoga

Vinyasa yoga is a more dynamic style of yoga that involves flowing movements and a focus on breath. This style can be more challenging, but can be particularly effective for reducing stress and anxiety.

Restorative Yoga

Restorative yoga involves holding gentle yoga poses for longer periods of time, often with the use of props such as blankets and bolsters. This style is particularly well-suited for those looking to promote relaxation and reduce stress.

Yoga Nidra

Yoga nidra is a guided relaxation technique that involves lying down and following a series of prompts to promote relaxation and reduce stress. This practice can be particularly effective for promoting sleep and reducing anxiety.

Progressive Muscle Relaxation

Progressive muscle relaxation is a relaxation technique that involves tensing and then relaxing different muscle groups throughout the body. This practice can be particularly effective for reducing physical symptoms of anxiety, such as muscle tension and pain.

Herbal remedies and supplements

Herbal remedies and supplements have been used for centuries to promote overall health and well-being, including in the treatment of anxiety disorders. While there is some evidence to suggest that certain herbs and supplements may be effective in managing anxiety symptoms, it is important to use caution when incorporating these remedies into a treatment plan. Below we will explore some of the herbal remedies and supplements commonly used for anxiety and their potential benefits and risks.

Herbs for Anxiety

Chamomile

Chamomile is a common herb that has been used for centuries to promote relaxation and reduce stress. Chamomile is often consumed as a tea and has been shown to have mild sedative effects. While chamomile is generally considered safe, it may interact with certain medications, so it is important to talk to a healthcare provider before using chamomile for anxiety.

Passionflower

Passionflower is another herb that has been used for centuries to promote relaxation and reduce anxiety. Passionflower is often consumed as a tea or taken in supplement form. While passionflower is generally considered safe, it may interact with certain medications, so it is important to talk to a healthcare provider before using passionflower for anxiety.

Valerian Root

Valerian root is an herb that has been used for centuries to promote relaxation and reduce anxiety. Valerian root is often consumed as a tea or taken in supplement form. While valerian root is generally considered safe, it may interact with certain medications, so it is important to talk to a healthcare provider before using valerian root for anxiety.

Supplements for Anxiety

Omega-3 Fatty Acids

Omega-3 fatty acids are a type of fat found in fish, nuts, and seeds. Omega-3 fatty acids have been shown to have anti-inflammatory effects and may help to reduce symptoms of anxiety. While omega-3 fatty acids are generally considered safe, high doses may increase the risk of bleeding, so it is important to talk to a healthcare provider before taking omega-3 supplements.

Magnesium

Magnesium is a mineral that plays a role in many bodily functions, including the regulation of mood and anxiety. Magnesium supplements may help to reduce symptoms of anxiety in some individuals. While magnesium is generally considered safe, high doses may cause diarrhea and other digestive issues, so it is important to talk to a healthcare provider before taking magnesium supplements.

L-Theanine

L-theanine is an amino acid found in tea leaves. L-theanine has been shown to promote relaxation and reduce anxiety in some individuals. While L-theanine is generally considered safe, it may interact with certain medications, so it is important to talk to a healthcare provider before taking L-theanine supplements.

Risks and Precautions

While herbal remedies and supplements may be effective in managing anxiety symptoms for some individuals, it is important to use caution when incorporating these remedies into a treatment plan. Some herbs and supplements may interact with certain medications, and high doses may cause adverse effects. It is important to talk to a healthcare provider before using any herbal remedies or supplements for anxiety.

Acupuncture and other holistic therapies

Anxiety disorders can have a profound impact on an individual's life, affecting their ability to function normally and enjoy everyday activities. While there are several evidence-based treatments available for anxiety disorders, some people prefer to explore alternative or complementary therapies to manage their symptoms. Acupuncture and other holistic therapies are two such options that have gained popularity in recent years.

Acupuncture is a traditional Chinese medicine technique that involves the insertion of thin needles into specific points on the body. According to traditional Chinese medicine, acupuncture helps to balance the body's energy, or qi, by unblocking or redirecting it. Western medicine explanations for the effectiveness of acupuncture suggest that the needles stimulate the nervous system, causing the release of endorphins and other chemicals that can reduce pain and promote relaxation.

Several studies have investigated the effectiveness of acupuncture for anxiety disorders. A 2018 systematic review and meta-analysis of 18 randomized controlled trials found that acupuncture was more effective than no treatment or sham acupuncture for reducing anxiety symptoms in people with generalized anxiety disorder. However, the authors noted that the quality of the evidence was low and more high-quality studies are needed to confirm these findings.

Other studies have also found mixed results when investigating the effectiveness of acupuncture for anxiety disorders. Some have found significant reductions in symptoms, while others have found no significant difference between acupuncture and placebo treatments. Additionally, it is important to note that acupuncture should be performed by a licensed and experienced practitioner to ensure safety and effectiveness.

Other holistic therapies that may be beneficial for anxiety disorders include mindfulness-based interventions, massage therapy, and aromatherapy. Mindfulness-based interventions, such as mindfulness-based stress reduction (MBSR) and mindfulness-based cognitive therapy (MBCT), have been shown to be effective in reducing anxiety symptoms in several studies. These interventions typically involve teaching individuals to focus on the present moment and accept their thoughts and feelings without judgment.

Massage therapy, which involves the manipulation of soft tissues in the body, has also been shown to be effective in reducing anxiety symptoms. A 2015 systematic review and meta-analysis of 12 randomized controlled trials found that massage therapy significantly reduced anxiety symptoms in people with generalized anxiety disorder, post-traumatic stress disorder, and other anxiety disorders.

Aromatherapy involves the use of essential oils to promote relaxation and reduce anxiety symptoms. While there is limited research on the effectiveness of aromatherapy for anxiety disorders, some studies have shown that certain essential oils, such as lavender and chamomile, may have a calming effect.

It is important to note that while holistic therapies may be effective in reducing anxiety symptoms for some individuals, they should not be used as a replacement for evidence-based treatments such as medication and psychotherapy. It is also important to consult with a healthcare professional before trying any new therapy, as some therapies may interact with medications or have other potential risks.

Chapter Nine

Self-Help Strategies

Anxiety disorders can be challenging to manage, but there are several self-help strategies that individuals can use to reduce their symptoms and improve their quality of life. These strategies can be used in combination with evidence-based treatments, such as medication and psychotherapy, or on their own as a way to manage mild symptoms.

One effective self-help strategy for anxiety disorders is exercise. Regular exercise has been shown to have a positive impact on mental health, including reducing symptoms of anxiety. Exercise releases endorphins, which are natural chemicals in the brain that can help to improve mood and reduce stress. Exercise can also help to improve sleep quality, which can be beneficial for individuals with anxiety disorders who may struggle with sleep disturbances.

Another self-help strategy is relaxation techniques, such as deep breathing, progressive muscle relaxation, and visualization. These techniques can be used to reduce symptoms of anxiety in the moment and can be helpful for individuals who experience sudden or intense symptoms. Deep breathing involves taking slow, deep breaths and focusing on the sensation of the breath in the body. Progressive muscle relaxation involves tensing and releasing different muscle groups in the body to promote relaxation. Visualization involves imagining a calming or peaceful scene to reduce stress and anxiety.

Mindfulness is another effective self-help strategy for anxiety disorders. Mindfulness involves focusing on the present moment and accepting thoughts and feelings without judgment. It can help individuals to reduce their reactivity to anxious thoughts and to develop a more positive relationship with their thoughts and feelings. There are several mindfulness-based interventions available, such as mindfulness-based stress reduction (MBSR) and mindfulness-based cognitive therapy (MBCT), which can be helpful for individuals with anxiety disorders.

In addition to these strategies, there are several lifestyle changes that can be beneficial for managing anxiety symptoms. These include getting enough sleep, eating a balanced diet, and reducing caffeine and alcohol intake. Adequate sleep is important for mental health and can help to reduce symptoms of anxiety. A balanced diet can provide the necessary nutrients to support mental health and reduce symptoms of anxiety. Caffeine and alcohol can both exacerbate symptoms of anxiety, so reducing or eliminating their intake may be helpful for some individuals.

Another self-help strategy is to practice self-care and prioritize activities that bring joy and relaxation. This can include engaging in hobbies, spending time with loved ones, and practicing gratitude. Engaging in activities that bring joy and relaxation can help to reduce stress and improve mood, which can be beneficial for managing anxiety symptoms.

It is important to note that while self-help strategies can be effective for managing anxiety symptoms, they should not be used as a replacement for evidence-based treatments. Individuals with severe or persistent symptoms should seek professional help from a healthcare provider. Additionally, it may be helpful to work with a therapist or counselor to develop a personalized self-help plan that is tailored to individual needs and preferences.

Breathing exercises and grounding techniques

Breathing exercises and grounding techniques are self-help strategies that can be used to manage anxiety disorders. These techniques have been found to be effective in reducing anxiety symptoms and promoting relaxation.

Breathing exercises involve focusing on your breath and regulating it in a specific way. One of the most popular breathing exercises is diaphragmatic breathing, also known as belly breathing. This technique involves taking slow, deep breaths from your diaphragm, rather than from your chest. To practice diaphragmatic breathing, lie down on your back or sit in a comfortable position, with one hand on your chest and the other on your belly. Inhale deeply through your nose, filling your belly with air and feeling your hand rise with each inhale. Exhale slowly through your mouth, feeling your belly fall with each exhale.

Another popular breathing exercise is the 4-7-8 technique, which involves inhaling for four seconds, holding your breath for seven seconds, and exhaling for eight seconds. Repeat this cycle several times, focusing on your breath and trying to relax your body.

Grounding techniques involve using your senses to bring your attention to the present moment and distract yourself from anxious thoughts. One grounding technique is the 5-4-3-2-1 exercise, which involves focusing on five things you can see, four things you can touch, three things you can hear, two things you can smell, and one thing you can taste. Another grounding technique is progressive muscle relaxation, which involves tensing and relaxing different muscle groups in your body, one at a time.

In addition to breathing exercises and grounding techniques, there are other self-help strategies that can be used to manage anxiety disorders. These include:

1. Exercise: Regular exercise has been found to be effective in reducing anxiety symptoms. Exercise can help to release endorphins, which are natural mood boosters, and also promote relaxation.

2. Mindfulness: Mindfulness involves bringing your attention to the present moment and accepting it without judgment. Mindfulness techniques can help to reduce anxiety symptoms and improve overall well-being.

3. Sleep hygiene: Good sleep hygiene involves practicing habits that promote restful sleep, such as avoiding caffeine and electronics before bedtime and creating a relaxing bedtime routine.

4. Nutrition: Eating a balanced diet that includes plenty of fruits, vegetables, whole grains, and lean proteins can help to promote overall well-being and reduce anxiety symptoms.

It is important to note that self-help strategies may not be enough to manage severe anxiety disorders, and individuals with severe anxiety symptoms may benefit from seeking professional help. However, these techniques can be a helpful complement to professional treatment, and can also be used to manage milder symptoms on a daily basis.

Building a support network

Anxiety disorders can be a challenging condition to manage, but with the right support network, people can learn to cope and thrive despite their symptoms. Building a support network can be a key aspect of recovery from anxiety disorders, helping individuals feel less alone, more connected, and more empowered to manage their symptoms.

One of the most important steps in building a support network is identifying the people in your life who can provide emotional and practical support. This might include family members, friends, partners, colleagues, or even mental health professionals. It can be helpful to think about the specific types of support you need, whether that's someone to talk to, someone to help with practical tasks, or someone to provide encouragement and motivation.

In addition to identifying people in your existing social network, it can also be helpful to seek out new sources of support. This might mean joining a support group for people with anxiety disorders, attending therapy, or participating in online forums or social media groups related to anxiety.

When building a support network, it's important to communicate openly and honestly with the people in your life about your condition and how they can best support you. This might mean explaining what anxiety feels like for you, what triggers your symptoms, and what coping strategies you find helpful. It can also be helpful to set boundaries and communicate your needs clearly, whether that means asking for space when you need it or asking for specific types of support.

Another key aspect of building a support network is self-care. While having supportive people in your life can be incredibly helpful, it's also important to prioritize your own needs and take steps to care for yourself. This might include practicing relaxation techniques, getting regular exercise, eating a healthy diet, getting enough sleep, and engaging in activities you enjoy.

Finally, it's important to remember that building a support network is an ongoing process. As your needs and circumstances change, you may need to adjust your support network accordingly. Don't be afraid to reach out for help or make changes as needed, and remember that you are not alone in your struggle with anxiety disorders.

Developing healthy coping mechanisms

Anxiety disorders can be a debilitating condition that affects millions of people worldwide. Although there is no cure for anxiety disorders, there are ways to manage the symptoms and improve the quality of life for those affected. One of the most important ways to do this is to develop healthy coping mechanisms.

Coping mechanisms are strategies used by individuals to manage stressful situations. Developing healthy coping mechanisms is crucial for individuals with anxiety disorders because it helps to reduce the impact of stressors on their mental and physical health. Below we will discuss the importance of developing healthy coping mechanisms and provide some examples of these strategies.

Firstly, it is important to understand that not all coping mechanisms are healthy. Some individuals may resort to unhealthy coping mechanisms such as substance abuse, overeating, or avoidance behavior. These behaviors may provide temporary relief from anxiety, but they can lead to long-term negative consequences such as addiction, obesity, or social isolation. Therefore, it is important to focus on healthy coping mechanisms that will promote long-term mental and physical well-being.

One of the most effective healthy coping mechanisms is relaxation techniques. These techniques can help to reduce anxiety by calming the mind and body. Examples of relaxation techniques include deep breathing exercises, progressive muscle relaxation, and visualization. Deep breathing exercises involve taking slow, deep breaths in through the nose and out through the mouth. Progressive muscle relaxation involves tensing and then relaxing each muscle group in the body, starting from the toes and working up to the head. Visualization involves imagining oneself in a peaceful, calm setting such as a beach or a forest.

Another healthy coping mechanism is exercise. Exercise is known to release endorphins, which are natural mood-boosting chemicals in the brain. It can also help to reduce muscle tension and promote relaxation. Exercise can take many forms, such as running, yoga, swimming, or weightlifting. The key is to find a form of exercise that is enjoyable and sustainable.

Social support is another important healthy coping mechanism. It is essential to have a network of supportive individuals who can provide emotional support and practical assistance when needed. This network may include family members, friends, therapists, or support groups. Connecting with others who have similar experiences can be particularly helpful in reducing feelings of isolation and providing a sense of community.

Meditation is another healthy coping mechanism that can be effective in reducing anxiety. Meditation involves focusing on the present moment and clearing the mind of distracting thoughts. It can help to increase mindfulness, which is the ability to observe one's thoughts and feelings without judgment. Meditation can take many forms, such as guided meditation, mantra meditation, or mindfulness meditation.

Another healthy coping mechanism is journaling. Writing down one's thoughts and feelings can help to process difficult emotions and reduce anxiety. Journaling can also provide a sense of control and organization in one's life. It can take many forms, such as free writing, gratitude journaling, or goal setting.

Finally, it is important to practice self-care as a healthy coping mechanism. Self-care involves taking care of oneself physically, emotionally, and mentally. This may include getting enough sleep, eating a healthy diet, engaging in hobbies or interests, or seeking professional help when needed. Self-care can also involve setting boundaries with others and prioritizing one's own needs.

Lifestyle changes and self-care

Anxiety disorders are highly prevalent and can significantly impact an individual's quality of life. Fortunately, there are many treatment options available to manage anxiety symptoms, including lifestyle changes and self-care practices. Below we will explore how lifestyle changes and self-care can help individuals with anxiety disorders.

Lifestyle changes and self-care are essential components of managing anxiety disorders. Lifestyle changes involve making modifications to one's daily routine to promote better overall health and well-being. Self-care practices are actions taken to improve one's mental, emotional, and physical health. Lifestyle changes and self-care practices can help individuals with anxiety disorders by reducing stress levels, promoting relaxation, and increasing overall feelings of well-being.

One of the most important lifestyle changes that individuals with anxiety disorders can make is to establish a regular sleep routine. Poor sleep can exacerbate anxiety symptoms, and getting enough restful sleep is essential for managing anxiety. Establishing a regular sleep routine involves going to bed and waking up at the same time each day, avoiding caffeine and electronics before bed, and creating a sleep-conducive environment.

Exercise is another important lifestyle change that can help manage anxiety symptoms. Regular exercise can reduce stress levels, boost mood, and improve overall physical health. Exercise can take many forms, including walking, running, swimming, yoga, and strength training. It is essential to find an exercise routine that one enjoys and can stick to consistently.

Diet is also an important factor to consider when managing anxiety. Some individuals with anxiety disorders may find that certain foods or beverages exacerbate their symptoms. It is essential to pay attention to how different foods affect one's anxiety and to make dietary changes accordingly. Some foods that may help manage anxiety symptoms include omega-3 fatty acids, whole grains, and foods high in magnesium.

In addition to lifestyle changes, there are many self-care practices that individuals with anxiety disorders can use to manage their symptoms. One effective self-care practice is mindfulness meditation. Mindfulness meditation involves focusing one's attention on the present moment and accepting one's thoughts and feelings without judgment. Regular practice of mindfulness meditation has been shown to reduce anxiety symptoms and improve overall well-being.

Breathing exercises are another effective self-care practice for managing anxiety symptoms. Deep breathing exercises can help to slow down the body's stress response and promote feelings of relaxation. One effective breathing exercise is the 4-7-8 breathing technique, which involves inhaling for four seconds, holding the breath for seven seconds, and exhaling for eight seconds.

In addition to these self-care practices, building a support network is essential for managing anxiety symptoms. This can include friends, family, support groups, or mental health professionals. A support network can provide a sense of belonging and help individuals with anxiety disorders feel less isolated.

Finally, developing healthy coping mechanisms is an essential aspect of managing anxiety disorders. Coping mechanisms can help individuals manage their symptoms when they arise. Some healthy coping mechanisms include journaling, listening to music, engaging in hobbies or creative pursuits, and practicing gratitude.

Chapter Ten

Managing Panic Attacks

Panic attacks are a common symptom of anxiety disorders, particularly Panic Disorder. Panic attacks are sudden and intense episodes of fear or anxiety that can last for a few minutes to several hours. During a panic attack, individuals may experience physical symptoms such as chest pain, sweating, trembling, and shortness of breath. Panic attacks can be extremely distressing and can have a significant impact on a person's daily life. However, there are several strategies that can help manage and reduce the severity of panic attacks.

The first step in managing panic attacks is to identify triggers. Triggers are situations, thoughts, or feelings that can cause a panic attack to occur. Common triggers include social situations, crowded places, public speaking, and stress. Once triggers are identified, individuals can work on avoiding or minimizing exposure to them.

Deep breathing exercises can also be helpful in managing panic attacks. When a panic attack occurs, it is common for individuals to hyperventilate or breathe rapidly, which can make symptoms worse. To counteract this, practicing deep breathing exercises can help regulate breathing and reduce the severity of symptoms. One technique is to inhale slowly through the nose for four seconds, hold the breath for seven seconds, and exhale slowly through the mouth for eight seconds.

Progressive muscle relaxation is another technique that can be used to manage panic attacks. This involves tensing and then relaxing different muscle groups in the body to reduce tension and promote relaxation. Starting with the feet and working up to the head, individuals can tense each muscle group for five seconds and then relax for 30 seconds.

Mindfulness techniques can also be effective in managing panic attacks. Mindfulness involves focusing on the present moment and observing thoughts and feelings without judgment. This can help individuals become more aware of their bodily sensations and feelings, which can help them manage panic attacks more effectively. Mindfulness meditation can be practiced for as little as 10 minutes per day and has been shown to have long-term benefits for anxiety and stress reduction.

Cognitive-behavioral therapy (CBT) is a type of therapy that can help individuals manage panic attacks. CBT focuses on identifying and changing negative thought patterns and behaviors that can contribute to anxiety. During therapy, individuals work with a therapist to develop coping strategies and learn techniques to manage anxiety symptoms.

Medications can also be used to manage panic attacks. Antidepressants and benzodiazepines are commonly prescribed for panic disorder. Antidepressants work by altering brain chemistry to regulate mood, while benzodiazepines work by enhancing the effects of a calming chemical in the brain. However, medications should only be taken under the supervision of a healthcare provider, as they can have side effects and can be addictive.

In addition to these strategies, lifestyle changes can also help manage panic attacks. Regular exercise, a healthy diet, and getting enough sleep can all contribute to overall mental and physical health. It is also important to avoid alcohol and caffeine, as these substances can trigger panic attacks.

Finally, building a support network can be helpful in managing panic attacks. This can include friends, family members, or a support group.

Talking to others who have experienced panic attacks can provide reassurance and help individuals feel less isolated.

Recognizing the signs of a panic attack

Panic attacks are sudden and intense feelings of fear, anxiety, or discomfort that can occur unexpectedly. They are a common symptom of anxiety disorders, including panic disorder, generalized anxiety disorder, and social anxiety disorder. Panic attacks can be frightening and overwhelming, and it is essential to recognize the signs and symptoms to seek appropriate help and support.

The signs and symptoms of a panic attack can vary from person to person. However, some common symptoms include:

Racing heartbeat or palpitations

Sweating or chills

Trembling or shaking

Shortness of breath or feeling like you are choking

Chest pain or discomfort

Nausea or abdominal distress

Feeling dizzy, lightheaded, or faint

Numbness or tingling sensations

Fear of losing control or going crazy

Fear of dying

These symptoms can occur suddenly and intensely, typically peaking within ten minutes and lasting for up to an hour. Panic attacks can occur at any time, including during sleep, and can be triggered by specific situations or activities.

Recognizing the signs and symptoms of a panic attack is crucial in managing anxiety and preventing the development of more severe conditions such as panic disorder. Panic attacks can often be mistaken for a heart attack or other medical emergency, leading to unnecessary hospital visits and anxiety.

If you experience panic attacks frequently, it is important to seek help from a mental health professional who can assess your symptoms and provide appropriate treatment. Several treatments are available to manage and prevent panic attacks, including therapy and medications.

Cognitive-behavioral therapy (CBT) is an evidence-based treatment that can help individuals understand and manage their thoughts and emotions during a panic attack. Exposure therapy is another approach that gradually exposes individuals to their feared situations, helping them develop coping strategies and decrease anxiety.

Medications such as antidepressants, benzodiazepines, and beta-blockers may also be prescribed to manage panic attacks. These medications work by reducing symptoms of anxiety and helping individuals feel more relaxed.

In addition to seeking professional help, there are several self-help strategies that can be implemented to manage panic attacks. These strategies include deep breathing exercises, progressive muscle relaxation, and mindfulness techniques.

Physical exercise, healthy eating, and reducing caffeine and alcohol intake can also help manage panic attacks. Engaging in hobbies and activities that bring joy and relaxation can also improve overall well-being and reduce anxiety.

Strategies for coping during a panic attack

Strategies for Coping During a Panic Attack

Panic attacks can be a terrifying experience, characterized by sudden and intense feelings of fear, racing heart rate, shortness of breath, and other physical symptoms. These attacks can happen unexpectedly, making it difficult to manage the symptoms and causing significant distress. However, there are strategies that can help individuals cope during a panic attack and reduce the likelihood of future attacks. Below we will explore some of these strategies and provide guidance on how to manage a panic attack.

Breathing exercises

Breathing exercises can help individuals during a panic attack by slowing down their heart rate and reducing physical tension. One common technique is diaphragmatic breathing, which involves breathing deeply from the belly. To practice this technique, individuals should sit or lie down in a comfortable position, place one hand on their chest and the other on their belly, and take slow, deep breaths through their nose. As they inhale, they should feel their belly expand, and as they exhale, they should feel their belly contract. This exercise can be repeated for several minutes until the individual feels more relaxed.

Muscle relaxation

Muscle relaxation exercises can help individuals reduce tension in their muscles and alleviate physical symptoms of panic attacks. One technique is progressive muscle relaxation, which involves tensing and relaxing each muscle group in the body, starting from the toes and working up to the head. To practice this technique, individuals should sit or lie down in a comfortable position, close their eyes, and focus on tensing one muscle group for a few seconds before releasing the tension and relaxing the muscle. This exercise can be repeated for several minutes until the individual feels more relaxed.

Mindfulness

Mindfulness can help individuals cope with the emotional distress that accompanies panic attacks. Mindfulness involves paying attention to the present moment without judgment, and it can help individuals become more aware of their thoughts and feelings. One technique is to focus on the physical sensations in the body during a panic attack, without becoming overwhelmed by the thoughts and emotions that accompany the attack. By focusing on the present moment and staying grounded in their body, individuals can reduce the intensity of their panic symptoms.

Guided imagery

Guided imagery involves using mental images to create a sense of relaxation and calm. During a panic attack, individuals can use guided imagery to visualize a calming scene, such as a beach or a forest. To practice this technique, individuals should sit or lie down in a comfortable position, close their eyes, and visualize themselves in a calming environment. They can also focus on other sensory details, such as the sound of the waves or the smell of the forest. This technique can help individuals shift their focus away from the panic attack and reduce their physical symptoms.

Seeking support

During a panic attack, it can be helpful to seek support from a trusted friend or family member. These individuals can provide emotional support and help the individual feel less isolated during the attack. Additionally, individuals can seek support from mental health professionals, such as therapists or counselors, who can provide more specialized guidance on managing panic attacks and reducing anxiety symptoms.

Preventing future panic attacks

Panic attacks can be a terrifying experience, characterized by sudden and intense feelings of fear and apprehension. While panic attacks can be a symptom of different anxiety disorders, such as panic disorder and generalized anxiety disorder, they can also occur in people who have no history of anxiety. Preventing future panic attacks involves understanding their triggers, developing healthy coping strategies, and seeking professional help when necessary.

One of the first steps in preventing future panic attacks is to identify their triggers. Common triggers include stress, caffeine, certain medications, and a lack of sleep. Keeping a journal to record the details of each panic attack, such as what was happening before the attack and how you felt, can help identify potential triggers. Once you have identified your triggers, you can take steps to avoid them or manage them better.

Another important step in preventing future panic attacks is to develop healthy coping strategies. This can involve various techniques such as deep breathing, progressive muscle relaxation, and mindfulness meditation. It is also important to engage in regular physical activity, as exercise is known to reduce stress and improve mood. Additionally, maintaining a healthy diet and getting enough sleep can also be beneficial in preventing panic attacks.

In addition to developing healthy coping strategies, seeking professional help can also be an important part of preventing future panic attacks. A mental health professional can work with you to develop a personalized treatment plan that may include therapy, medication, or a combination of both. Cognitive-behavioral therapy (CBT) is a common type of therapy used to treat panic disorder, as it helps individuals learn to identify and change negative thought patterns and behaviors that may contribute to panic attacks.

In some cases, medication may be prescribed to help prevent future panic attacks. Antidepressants and benzodiazepines are two types of medications commonly used to treat panic disorder. Antidepressants work by regulating serotonin and norepinephrine levels in the brain, while benzodiazepines act as sedatives to help reduce anxiety. It is important to work closely with a healthcare provider to determine the appropriate medication and dosage.

It is also important to note that prevention of future panic attacks may not be possible in all cases. Some individuals may continue to experience panic attacks despite making healthy lifestyle changes and receiving professional treatment. However, with appropriate treatment and support, it is possible to manage panic attacks and reduce their frequency and intensity.

Chapter Eleven

Overcoming Social Anxiety

Social anxiety disorder, also known as social phobia, is a type of anxiety disorder that affects millions of people worldwide. It is characterized by an intense fear of social situations or scrutiny, which can cause individuals to avoid social interactions altogether. Social anxiety can have a significant impact on an individual's life, causing them to miss out on important events, limit their career opportunities, and negatively affect their relationships. Fortunately, social anxiety is a treatable condition, and with the right approach, individuals can overcome it and lead a fulfilling life.

One of the first steps in overcoming social anxiety is understanding the condition and recognizing the signs. Social anxiety can manifest in various ways, including fear of public speaking, fear of being judged or criticized, fear of eating or drinking in public, fear of using public restrooms, fear of attending social gatherings, and fear of initiating conversations. These fears can be debilitating and can cause intense physical symptoms, including trembling, sweating, heart palpitations, and nausea.

The next step is seeking professional help. Cognitive-behavioral therapy (CBT) is a highly effective treatment for social anxiety. In CBT, individuals learn to identify and change negative thought patterns that contribute to their anxiety. They also learn coping strategies to help them manage their symptoms in social situations. Exposure therapy is also commonly used to treat social anxiety, where individuals are gradually exposed to the situations that cause them anxiety. This exposure is done in a controlled and safe environment, allowing individuals to learn how to manage their anxiety effectively.

Medication can also be used in the treatment of social anxiety, including selective serotonin reuptake inhibitors (SSRIs) and benzodiazepines. SSRIs work by increasing levels of serotonin in the brain, which can help reduce anxiety symptoms. Benzodiazepines work by enhancing the effects of the neurotransmitter GABA, which can help calm the nervous system.

In addition to professional help, there are several self-help strategies that individuals with social anxiety can use to overcome their symptoms. These include practicing relaxation techniques such as deep breathing, meditation, and yoga. Regular exercise has also been shown to be beneficial in reducing anxiety symptoms. Developing a support network of friends and family who understand and support your struggles can also be helpful.

It is also essential to challenge negative beliefs and self-talk that contribute to social anxiety. Instead of focusing on the worst-case scenario, try to challenge these thoughts by asking yourself if they are realistic or rational. Engaging in positive self-talk and affirmations can also be helpful in changing negative beliefs.

Challenging negative thoughts and beliefs

Anxiety disorders can have a significant impact on an individual's thoughts, feelings, and behavior. Negative thoughts and beliefs can exacerbate anxiety symptoms and lead to a cycle of worry and fear. One effective strategy for managing anxiety is to challenge negative thoughts and beliefs.

Negative thoughts can take many forms, including catastrophizing, personalizing, and overgeneralizing. Catastrophizing involves imagining the worst possible outcome of a situation. For example, an individual with social anxiety might think, "If I stutter during this presentation, everyone will laugh at me and I'll never be able to show my face in public again." Personalizing involves taking responsibility for things that are outside of one's control. For example, an individual with social anxiety might think, "If my friend doesn't have a good time at this party, it will be my fault." Overgeneralizing involves making sweeping negative statements about oneself or the world based on limited evidence. For example, an individual with social anxiety might think, "I always make a fool of myself in social situations."

Challenging negative thoughts involves examining the evidence for and against a particular thought or belief. This can help individuals to develop a more balanced and realistic perspective. For example, an individual with social anxiety might challenge the thought, "If I stutter during this presentation, everyone will laugh at me and I'll never be able to show my face in public again." They might ask themselves, "What is the evidence for this thought?" They might then consider the fact that many people stutter from time to time and that it is unlikely that everyone in the room will laugh. They might also consider the fact that they have given presentations before without experiencing the worst possible outcome.

Another effective strategy for challenging negative thoughts is to consider the impact of the thought. Negative thoughts can have a powerful impact on an individual's emotions and behavior. By recognizing the impact of negative thoughts, individuals can develop a motivation to challenge them. For example, an individual with social anxiety might think, "If I stutter during this presentation, everyone will laugh at me and I'll never be able to show my face in public again." They might then consider how this thought makes them feel - anxious, embarrassed, and ashamed. They might also consider how this thought is likely to impact their behavior - they might avoid giving presentations in the future, which could limit their professional opportunities.

In addition to challenging negative thoughts, individuals can develop more positive and realistic beliefs. This can involve developing a more compassionate and realistic view of oneself and others. For example, an individual with social anxiety might challenge the thought, "I always make a fool of myself in social situations." They might replace this thought with a more positive and realistic belief, such as, "I sometimes feel nervous in social situations, but I also have many positive qualities that I can bring to these situations." They might also challenge the belief that others are judging them harshly by reminding themselves that most people are focused on their own concerns and are not paying close attention to their every move.

There are several techniques that individuals can use to challenge negative thoughts and beliefs. One effective technique is to write down the negative thought and then generate evidence for and against it. This can help individuals to see the thought more objectively and develop a more balanced perspective. Another technique is to use a thought record, which involves recording negative thoughts, emotions, and behaviors and then challenging the thoughts using evidence and alternative beliefs. Mindfulness meditation can also be helpful in developing a more objective and non-judgmental perspective on one's thoughts and emotions.

Developing effective communication skills

Anxiety disorders can have a profound impact on an individual's ability to communicate effectively with others. Those who struggle with anxiety may experience a range of symptoms, including social avoidance, self-consciousness, and difficulty expressing themselves. As a result, it is important for individuals with anxiety to develop effective communication skills in order to improve their quality of life and relationships with others.

One key aspect of effective communication is assertiveness. This involves expressing one's needs and opinions in a clear and direct manner while also respecting the needs and opinions of others. For individuals with anxiety, assertiveness can be particularly challenging as they may struggle with feelings of self-doubt and fear of rejection. However, learning assertiveness skills can help individuals build confidence in their ability to communicate effectively and advocate for themselves in social situations.

Another important aspect of effective communication is active listening. This involves paying attention to the speaker and demonstrating a willingness to understand their perspective. Active listening can help individuals build stronger connections with others and avoid misunderstandings or conflicts. For individuals with anxiety, active listening can also help them overcome feelings of self-consciousness and reduce social anxiety.

In addition to assertiveness and active listening, individuals with anxiety may also benefit from learning relaxation techniques to manage their symptoms during social interactions. Deep breathing, progressive muscle relaxation, and mindfulness meditation can all be effective strategies for reducing anxiety and improving one's ability to communicate with others.

Finally, seeking professional help from a therapist or counselor can also be an effective way to improve communication skills and overcome anxiety. Therapists can help individuals identify underlying causes of their anxiety and develop strategies to manage their symptoms. They can also provide guidance and support as individuals work to build more effective communication skills.

Building self-confidence and self-esteem

Anxiety disorders can significantly impact an individual's self-confidence and self-esteem. It can cause a person to feel constantly on edge, worried, and self-conscious, which can lead to negative beliefs about themselves and their abilities. Building self-confidence and self-esteem is an important part of managing anxiety disorders and improving overall mental health.

Self-confidence refers to a person's belief in their abilities and skills. Self-esteem refers to how a person feels about themselves overall. Both are important components of mental health and can be impacted by anxiety disorders. Individuals with anxiety disorders may feel like they are not capable of handling certain situations or may feel like they are constantly being judged by others. These negative thoughts can lead to a decrease in self-confidence and self-esteem.

There are several strategies that individuals with anxiety disorders can use to build self-confidence and self-esteem. One of the most effective ways is to challenge negative thoughts and beliefs. When an individual experiences negative thoughts, such as "I'm not good enough" or "I'm going to fail," it can be helpful to question the validity of these thoughts. Often, these thoughts are not based on facts but rather on anxiety and fear. By questioning these thoughts, individuals can begin to see themselves in a more positive light and build self-confidence.

Another important strategy for building self-confidence and self-esteem is to practice self-care. This involves taking care of oneself physically, emotionally, and mentally. Self-care can include activities such as exercise, getting enough sleep, eating a healthy diet, and engaging in activities that bring joy and relaxation. By taking care of oneself, individuals can improve their overall well-being and feel more confident in their abilities.

Developing effective communication skills is also an important aspect of building self-confidence and self-esteem. Communication skills involve being able to express oneself clearly and assertively while also being able to listen actively to others. Effective communication can help individuals feel more confident in their ability to express themselves and can lead to stronger relationships with others.

In addition to these strategies, setting achievable goals and celebrating accomplishments can also help build self-confidence and self-esteem. Setting goals, both big and small, can give individuals a sense of purpose and direction. When goals are achieved, it can lead to a sense of accomplishment and a boost in self-confidence.

It is important to note that building self-confidence and self-esteem is not an overnight process. It takes time and effort to challenge negative thoughts and beliefs, practice self-care, develop effective communication skills, and set achievable goals. It is also important to seek support from others, such as friends, family, or a mental health professional, as they can provide encouragement and guidance throughout the process.

Chapter Twelve

Confronting Specific Phobias

Confronting specific phobias can be a daunting task for many individuals who suffer from anxiety disorders. Specific phobias are intense and irrational fears of certain objects or situations that can lead to avoidance behaviors and significant distress. However, there are several strategies and techniques that can be used to confront and overcome specific phobias.

The first step in confronting specific phobias is to understand the nature of the phobia itself. This may involve learning more about the specific object or situation that triggers the phobia, as well as any underlying beliefs or thought patterns that may be contributing to the fear. For example, someone with a fear of flying may have underlying beliefs about the safety of air travel or the lack of control they feel during a flight.

Once the nature of the phobia is understood, a therapist can work with the individual to develop a hierarchy of fear, which involves identifying and ranking situations or stimuli that trigger the phobia from least to most anxiety-provoking. This hierarchy can then be used as a guide for exposure therapy, a type of behavioral therapy that involves gradually exposing the individual to the feared stimuli or situations in a controlled and safe environment.

Exposure therapy can take many forms, depending on the nature of the phobia. For example, someone with a fear of spiders may start by looking at pictures of spiders, then progress to being in the same room as a spider in a cage, and eventually holding a spider. The goal of exposure therapy is to help the individual develop new associations with the feared object or situation, and to learn that they can tolerate the anxiety that arises.

In addition to exposure therapy, cognitive-behavioral therapy (CBT) can also be helpful in confronting specific phobias. CBT involves identifying and challenging negative thoughts and beliefs about the feared object or situation, and replacing them with more realistic and helpful thoughts. For example, someone with a fear of public speaking may have negative thoughts such as "I will embarrass myself" or "I will forget my words." Through CBT, they can learn to challenge these thoughts and replace them with more realistic thoughts such as "It's normal to feel nervous before a speech" or "I have prepared and practiced, and I can do this."

Other strategies for confronting specific phobias may include relaxation techniques, such as deep breathing or progressive muscle relaxation, to help manage anxiety during exposure therapy. Support from family and friends can also be helpful, as can participating in support groups with others who share the same phobia.

It is important to note that confronting specific phobias can be a gradual process, and there may be setbacks along the way. It is also important to work with a qualified therapist who has experience in treating anxiety disorders, as they can provide guidance and support throughout the process.

Identifying the root cause of phobias

Identifying the root cause of phobias can be an important step towards overcoming these intense and irrational fears. A phobia is an excessive and persistent fear of a specific object, situation, or activity, and it can significantly interfere with a person's daily life. While the exact cause of phobias is not fully understood, there are several theories and factors that can contribute to their development.

One possible root cause of phobias is a traumatic event or experience. For example, if someone had a frightening encounter with a dog in childhood, they may develop a persistent fear of dogs. This fear can become increasingly intense over time and may generalize to other dogs or similar animals. Similarly, if someone experiences a panic attack or intense anxiety in a particular situation, such as flying or driving, they may develop a phobia of that situation.

Another possible root cause of phobias is a learned behavior. This can occur through direct or indirect observation of others' reactions to a particular object or situation. For example, if a child sees their parent's extreme fear of spiders, they may learn to associate spiders with danger and develop a phobia. Additionally, cultural or societal factors can also influence the development of phobias. For instance, in some cultures, snakes are associated with evil or danger, which can contribute to the development of a snake phobia.

There is also evidence to suggest that genetic and biological factors may play a role in the development of phobias. Research has shown that phobias can run in families, and there may be a genetic predisposition to anxiety disorders. Additionally, brain chemistry and neurobiological factors may also contribute to the development of phobias.

Regardless of the root cause of a phobia, it is important to seek treatment to manage symptoms and improve quality of life. Treatment for phobias typically involves a combination of therapy and medication.

Cognitive-behavioral therapy (CBT) is a common and effective treatment for phobias. CBT helps individuals identify and challenge negative thought patterns and beliefs that contribute to their fear. Additionally, exposure therapy is a form of CBT that involves gradually exposing the individual to the feared object or situation in a safe and controlled environment. Through repeated exposure, the person can learn to face their fear and gradually reduce anxiety.

In some cases, medication may also be prescribed to help manage symptoms of phobias. Antidepressants and anti-anxiety medications can be helpful in reducing the severity of symptoms and improving overall functioning.

Other treatment options for phobias may include relaxation techniques, such as deep breathing or progressive muscle relaxation, and mindfulness-based interventions, such as meditation. These practices can help individuals manage symptoms of anxiety and stress, and develop a greater sense of self-awareness and control over their thoughts and emotions.

Exposure therapy and systematic desensitization

Exposure therapy and systematic desensitization are two commonly used treatment options for specific phobias, which are a type of anxiety disorder. These therapies aim to reduce or eliminate the fear and avoidance associated with a specific object or situation.

Exposure therapy involves gradually exposing the person to the feared object or situation in a safe and controlled environment. This exposure can be in vivo, meaning in the actual presence of the feared object or situation, or imaginal, where the person is asked to imagine the feared situation in their mind. The exposure is done in a systematic way, starting with less anxiety-provoking situations and progressing to more challenging situations. The person is encouraged to confront their fear and resist the urge to avoid the feared object or situation.

Systematic desensitization is a type of exposure therapy that involves pairing relaxation techniques with exposure to the feared object or situation. The person is taught relaxation techniques, such as deep breathing or progressive muscle relaxation, and then asked to imagine the feared situation while using these relaxation techniques. The imagined situation is gradually made more and more intense until the person can imagine the feared situation without experiencing high levels of anxiety.

Both exposure therapy and systematic desensitization are effective in treating specific phobias. These therapies work by helping the person to confront their fear and learn that the feared object or situation is not actually dangerous. Through repeated exposure, the person learns that they can tolerate the anxiety associated with the feared object or situation and that their fear will decrease over time.

It is important to note that exposure therapy and systematic desensitization should only be done with the guidance of a trained mental health professional. These therapies can be difficult and uncomfortable, and it is important that the person is supported throughout the process. Additionally, these therapies may not be appropriate for everyone and alternative treatment options should be explored if the person is unable or unwilling to participate in these therapies.

In addition to exposure therapy and systematic desensitization, other treatment options for specific phobias include cognitive-behavioral therapy (CBT) and medication. CBT focuses on changing the negative thoughts and beliefs associated with the feared object or situation, while medication, such as beta-blockers or anti-anxiety medication, can help to reduce the physical symptoms of anxiety.

Coping strategies for facing fears

Coping strategies for facing fears are essential for people who struggle with anxiety disorders, particularly those who have specific phobias. Facing your fears can be a challenging and uncomfortable experience, but it is often necessary to overcome them and live a fulfilling life. Below we will explore some effective coping strategies for facing fears.

One of the most effective coping strategies for facing fears is exposure therapy. Exposure therapy involves gradually exposing yourself to the feared object or situation until you can face it without experiencing intense fear. The exposure can be done in various ways, such as in vivo exposure, where you face the feared object or situation in real life, or imaginal exposure, where you imagine the feared object or situation in your mind. Exposure therapy is usually conducted under the guidance of a trained therapist who will help you to develop a hierarchy of feared situations and gradually expose you to them.

Another effective coping strategy for facing fears is systematic desensitization. This approach involves pairing relaxation techniques with exposure to the feared object or situation. You first learn relaxation techniques such as deep breathing, progressive muscle relaxation, or visualization. Then, you gradually expose yourself to the feared object or situation while practicing the relaxation techniques. The idea is that the relaxation techniques help you to cope with the anxiety and reduce your fear response.

Another coping strategy for facing fears is cognitive restructuring. This approach involves challenging negative thoughts and beliefs that contribute to your fears. For example, if you have a fear of public speaking, you may believe that you will embarrass yourself or that people will judge you harshly. Cognitive restructuring involves examining these beliefs and finding evidence to support or challenge them. You may find that there is little evidence to support your fears, or that there are alternative explanations for the situation.

Mindfulness and meditation are also effective coping strategies for facing fears. Mindfulness involves being present in the moment and accepting your thoughts and feelings without judgment. Meditation involves focusing your attention on a specific object or sensation, such as your breath. Both mindfulness and meditation can help you to become more aware of your thoughts and feelings and develop a sense of control over them. This can help to reduce anxiety and improve your ability to face your fears.

Building a support network is another important coping strategy for facing fears. Talking to friends, family, or a support group can help you to feel understood and validated. They can also provide you with practical support and encouragement as you face your fears. You may also benefit from seeking professional help from a therapist or counselor who can help you to develop effective coping strategies and provide emotional support.

Developing healthy coping mechanisms is another important strategy for facing fears. This can include exercise, healthy eating, getting enough sleep, and practicing self-care. These activities can help you to manage stress and reduce anxiety, making it easier to face your fears.

Chapter Thirteen

Parenting a Child with Anxiety

Anxiety disorders are the most common mental health issues in children and adolescents, affecting up to 25% of young people. As a parent, it can be challenging to see your child struggle with anxiety. However, there are many ways that you can support your child and help them manage their anxiety. Below we will discuss some strategies that parents can use to help their children cope with anxiety.

The first step in helping a child with anxiety is to recognize the signs. Symptoms of anxiety can manifest in many ways, including physical symptoms such as headaches or stomach aches, behavioral symptoms such as avoidance or clinginess, and emotional symptoms such as fear or worry. If you suspect that your child may be experiencing anxiety, it is important to seek professional help. A mental health professional can help diagnose the anxiety disorder and recommend appropriate treatment.

One of the most effective treatments for childhood anxiety is cognitive-behavioral therapy (CBT). CBT is a form of therapy that helps children identify and change negative thought patterns and behaviors that contribute to anxiety. In CBT, children learn skills such as relaxation techniques, problem-solving, and assertiveness training.

As a parent, you can support your child's CBT treatment by reinforcing the skills they learn in therapy. You can practice relaxation techniques with your child, encourage them to problem-solve, and help them communicate their needs assertively. Additionally, you can work with your child's therapist to develop a plan for coping with anxiety symptoms at home and school.

Another important aspect of supporting a child with anxiety is creating a safe and predictable environment. Children with anxiety may feel more comfortable and secure when they know what to expect. You can create a routine for your child that includes regular meals, bedtime, and activities. Additionally, you can provide a safe space for your child to retreat to when they feel overwhelmed by anxiety.

It is also important to encourage your child to engage in activities that they enjoy. Hobbies and interests can provide a sense of accomplishment and joy that can counteract the negative effects of anxiety. Additionally, participating in activities with other children can help your child develop social skills and a sense of belonging.

Parents can also model healthy coping strategies for their children. If you struggle with anxiety yourself, it can be helpful to share your experiences with your child and model healthy ways to manage anxiety symptoms. This can include practicing relaxation techniques, exercising, and seeking support from friends and family.

Finally, it is important to remember that every child is unique, and what works for one child may not work for another. It may take some trial and error to find the best strategies for helping your child manage their anxiety. However, with patience, support, and professional help, children with anxiety can learn to manage their symptoms and lead fulfilling lives.

Recognizing anxiety symptoms in children

Anxiety disorders are not limited to adults and can also affect children. In fact, anxiety is the most common mental health issue in children and adolescents, with around one in eight children experiencing an anxiety disorder at some point in their life. It is essential for parents and caregivers to recognize the signs of anxiety in children to provide them with the appropriate support and treatment.

One of the most common symptoms of anxiety in children is excessive worry. Children with anxiety may worry about things that are not significant to their peers, such as being separated from their parents or being late for school. They may also worry about potential danger and harm, which can lead to a reluctance to participate in activities or leave the house. Other signs of anxiety in children include restlessness, irritability, trouble sleeping, and physical symptoms such as headaches and stomachaches.

Parents and caregivers can also look for behavioral changes in children with anxiety. These can include avoidance of certain situations or people, refusal to go to school or engage in social activities, and compulsive behaviors such as hand washing or checking doors and windows. Children with anxiety may also become clingy and seek constant reassurance from their parents.

It is essential to understand that anxiety in children can manifest in different ways depending on the child's age and development. Young children may have difficulty verbalizing their emotions and may express anxiety through physical symptoms or behavioral changes. Older children and adolescents may be able to communicate their worries more effectively but may also experience more complex emotions such as embarrassment or shame.

Recognizing anxiety symptoms in children is the first step in helping them manage their anxiety. It is essential to seek professional help if parents or caregivers suspect that their child has an anxiety disorder. A mental health professional can assess the child's symptoms and provide appropriate treatment and support.

Parents and caregivers can also help children manage their anxiety by providing a supportive and calm environment. Encouraging open communication and active listening can help children feel heard and understood. It is also essential to provide children with a routine and structure, which can help them feel more in control and reduce anxiety.

Parents and caregivers can also teach children relaxation techniques such as deep breathing and mindfulness to help them cope with anxiety symptoms. Exercise and physical activity can also be helpful in managing anxiety in children. Encouraging children to engage in activities they enjoy and helping them develop coping strategies can help them build resilience and manage their anxiety.

Supporting your child through treatment

Anxiety disorders are a common mental health issue that can affect people of all ages, including children. As a parent, it can be difficult to see your child struggle with anxiety, but there are steps you can take to support them through treatment and help them manage their symptoms. Here are some tips for supporting your child through anxiety treatment:

1. Educate yourself: The first step in supporting your child is to educate yourself about anxiety disorders. Learn about the different types of anxiety disorders, the symptoms, and the treatments available. This can help you understand what your child is going through and how you can best support them.

2. Listen to your child: It's important to listen to your child and validate their feelings. Encourage them to express their thoughts and feelings, and let them know that you are there to support them. It's also important to avoid minimizing their anxiety or telling them to "just relax."

3. Be patient: Recovery from anxiety can be a slow process, so it's important to be patient and not expect instant results. Encourage your child to stick with their treatment and remind them that progress can take time.

4. Encourage healthy habits: Encourage your child to maintain healthy habits, such as getting enough sleep, eating a balanced diet, and engaging in physical activity. These habits can help improve overall wellbeing and reduce anxiety symptoms.

5. Avoid avoidance: Avoidance can reinforce anxiety, so it's important to encourage your child to face their fears and gradually work on exposure to anxiety-provoking situations. This can be done through exposure therapy, which involves gradually exposing the child to their fears in a safe and controlled environment.

6. Involve the school: If your child is experiencing anxiety, it may be helpful to involve the school in their treatment. Talk to your child's teachers and guidance counselors to ensure that they are aware of your child's anxiety and to discuss strategies for supporting them in the classroom.

7. Seek professional help: If your child's anxiety is interfering with their daily life, it may be time to seek professional help. A mental health professional, such as a psychologist or psychiatrist, can work with your child to develop an individualized treatment plan that may include therapy, medication, or a combination of both.

8. Model healthy coping strategies: Children often learn by example, so it's important to model healthy coping strategies. Practice mindfulness, engage in relaxation techniques, and practice healthy communication skills. This can help your child learn effective coping strategies that they can use in their own lives.

9. Practice self-care: Caring for a child with anxiety can be stressful, so it's important to practice self-care. Take time for yourself to recharge and practice stress-reducing activities such as exercise, meditation, or spending time with friends and family.

Encouraging resilience and coping skills

Anxiety disorders can be particularly challenging for children, as they are still developing their coping skills and emotional regulation abilities. As a parent or caregiver, it can be difficult to see your child struggling with anxiety. However, there are strategies that can be used to encourage resilience and coping skills in children with anxiety.

The first step is to provide a supportive environment. This means being present and attentive to your child's needs, while also providing them with a sense of safety and security. Children with anxiety often feel overwhelmed and frightened, so it is important to create a calm and reassuring environment for them. This can involve spending quality time with your child, listening to their concerns, and providing emotional support.

It is also important to model healthy coping skills. Children learn by example, so it is important to demonstrate effective ways to cope with stress and anxiety. This can include engaging in self-care activities such as exercise, mindfulness, or relaxation techniques. When your child sees you using these strategies, they are more likely to incorporate them into their own coping repertoire.

Another strategy is to encourage your child to develop problem-solving skills. This involves teaching them to identify the source of their anxiety and come up with practical solutions to address it. For example, if your child is anxious about making friends at school, you could brainstorm together about ways to initiate conversations or activities with other children. This can help to build their confidence and reduce their anxiety in the long term.

Social support is also important for children with anxiety. Encouraging your child to connect with friends or family members who provide positive support can be beneficial. It is also helpful to seek out support groups or therapy for children with anxiety, as they can provide a safe and supportive environment for children to discuss their fears and learn coping skills.

Teaching your child to reframe negative thoughts is another effective strategy for building resilience. Children with anxiety often have negative thoughts about themselves, their abilities, or their future. By teaching them to recognize these thoughts and replace them with positive, realistic ones, they can learn to reframe their anxiety and build a more positive self-image.

Finally, it is important to celebrate your child's successes, no matter how small. This can help to build their self-esteem and reinforce their coping skills. When your child successfully copes with a challenging situation, such as speaking in front of a group or making a new friend, be sure to acknowledge and celebrate their accomplishment.

Chapter Fourteen

Anxiety in Adolescents

Anxiety is a common problem among adolescents. In fact, it is estimated that one in three adolescents will experience an anxiety disorder during their teenage years. Anxiety can be a normal part of the adolescent experience, but it can also become debilitating if left untreated. Below we will explore the causes and symptoms of anxiety in adolescents, as well as effective treatment options.

Causes of Anxiety in Adolescents

There is no single cause of anxiety in adolescents, but it is believed to be the result of a combination of genetic, environmental, and developmental factors. Adolescents who have a family history of anxiety or other mental health disorders may be at a higher risk of developing anxiety. Environmental factors such as stress, trauma, and abuse can also contribute to the development of anxiety in adolescents. Additionally, changes in brain chemistry and hormonal imbalances during puberty can play a role in the development of anxiety.

Symptoms of Anxiety in Adolescents

The symptoms of anxiety in adolescents can vary from person to person, but they often include physical, emotional, and behavioral changes. Physical symptoms may include rapid heartbeat, sweating, shaking, and shortness of breath. Emotional symptoms may include feelings of fear, worry, or panic. Behavioral symptoms may include avoidance of certain situations or activities, as well as changes in sleep or eating habits.

Anxiety can also have a negative impact on an adolescent's academic and social functioning. They may have difficulty concentrating in school or participating in social activities. It is not uncommon for adolescents with anxiety to miss school or avoid social events altogether.

Treatment Options

Fortunately, there are many effective treatment options for anxiety in adolescents. The most commonly used treatments are therapy and medication.

Therapy

Cognitive-behavioral therapy (CBT) is the most widely used therapy for anxiety in adolescents. This therapy focuses on identifying negative thought patterns and replacing them with positive, rational thoughts. CBT also involves exposure therapy, which gradually exposes the adolescent to the situation or object that causes anxiety until they are able to tolerate it without fear.

Another therapy that has shown promise for anxiety in adolescents is acceptance and commitment therapy (ACT). ACT focuses on helping adolescents accept their anxious thoughts and feelings rather than trying to eliminate them. The goal of ACT is to help adolescents develop new ways of responding to their anxiety so that it no longer controls their behavior.

Medication

Medication can also be effective in treating anxiety in adolescents, but it is typically used as a last resort after therapy has been unsuccessful. Antidepressants and anti-anxiety medications are commonly used to treat anxiety in adolescents. These medications can help reduce symptoms of anxiety, but they also have potential side effects and should be closely monitored by a healthcare provider.

Self-Help Strategies

In addition to therapy and medication, there are many self-help strategies that adolescents can use to manage their anxiety. These strategies include:

1. Regular exercise: Exercise is a natural mood booster and can help reduce symptoms of anxiety.

2. Deep breathing: Taking slow, deep breaths can help calm the body and reduce feelings of anxiety.

3. Mindfulness meditation: This practice involves focusing on the present moment and can help reduce anxiety.

4. Getting enough sleep: Adolescents need between 8-10 hours of sleep each night to function at their best. Lack of sleep can worsen symptoms of anxiety.

5. Avoiding caffeine and alcohol: Both caffeine and alcohol can increase symptoms of anxiety and should be avoided or limited.

Support from Family and Friends

Finally, it is important for adolescents with anxiety to receive support from their family and friends. Family members and friends can provide emotional support and help adolescents navigate their anxiety. Parents can also help their adolescents by encouraging healthy habits and providing a supportive environment at home.

The unique challenges of adolescent anxiety

Adolescence is a time of change and growth, marked by physical, emotional, and social transformations. It can also be a time of increased anxiety and stress, as adolescents navigate academic pressures, peer relationships, and personal identity. While it is normal for adolescents to experience some degree of anxiety, for some, it can become overwhelming and interfere with daily life. Below we will explore the unique challenges of adolescent anxiety and its impact on development.

One of the unique challenges of adolescent anxiety is the potential impact on academic performance. As adolescents face increased academic demands, the pressure to perform can contribute to anxiety. This anxiety can manifest as difficulty concentrating, decreased motivation, and a reluctance to attend school. These symptoms can lead to poor academic performance, which can further exacerbate anxiety and stress. Therefore, it is important for parents and educators to recognize the signs of anxiety in adolescents and provide support and resources to help them manage their anxiety.

Another challenge of adolescent anxiety is the impact on social relationships. Adolescents are navigating complex social dynamics and peer relationships, and anxiety can make it difficult to form and maintain these connections. Adolescents with anxiety may avoid social situations, struggle with communication, or fear being judged or rejected by their peers. This can contribute to feelings of isolation and loneliness, which can further fuel anxiety. It is essential for parents and educators to provide opportunities for adolescents to build positive relationships and to provide support and guidance on social skills and communication.

Adolescent anxiety can also impact personal identity and self-esteem. Adolescents are forming their sense of self and trying to establish their place in the world. Anxiety can interfere with this process, as it can cause self-doubt, negative self-talk, and a lack of confidence. This can lead to a negative impact on self-esteem and self-worth, which can have lasting effects on mental health and well-being. Therefore, it is important for parents and educators to help adolescents develop a positive self-image and to provide support and resources for managing anxiety.

Finally, adolescent anxiety can have long-term effects on mental health and well-being. Left unaddressed, anxiety in adolescence can lead to increased risk for depression, substance abuse, and other mental health disorders. It is essential for parents and educators to recognize the signs of anxiety in adolescents and to provide support and resources for managing anxiety, to promote mental health and well-being throughout adolescence and into adulthood.

Navigating school, social life, and extracurricular activities

Anxiety disorders can be especially challenging for adolescents as they navigate the pressures of school, social life, and extracurricular activities. The demands placed on teenagers can exacerbate feelings of stress and anxiety, leading to increased symptoms of anxiety disorders.

One of the primary challenges faced by adolescents with anxiety disorders is the pressure of academic performance. Many students experience anxiety related to grades, exams, and academic expectations. They may feel overwhelmed by the amount of work they have to do, leading to feelings of panic and dread. Additionally, they may struggle with procrastination and time management, which can exacerbate their anxiety symptoms.

Social life can also be a source of stress for adolescents with anxiety disorders. Teenagers often feel pressure to fit in with their peers, which can be difficult for those who struggle with social anxiety. They may feel self-conscious and worry about being judged by others, leading to avoidance of social situations and difficulty forming close friendships. This can create a cycle of isolation, which can further exacerbate anxiety symptoms.

Extracurricular activities can also be a source of stress for teenagers with anxiety disorders. Many adolescents feel pressure to participate in a variety of activities, such as sports, music, or clubs, in order to build their resumes and prepare for college. However, this can be overwhelming for those who struggle with anxiety, as it can lead to feelings of being overcommitted and spread too thin. Additionally, the pressure to perform well in these activities can exacerbate anxiety symptoms and lead to avoidance behaviors.

Navigating these challenges requires a combination of self-care strategies, support from family and friends, and professional treatment. Adolescents with anxiety disorders can benefit from learning stress-management techniques such as deep breathing, progressive muscle relaxation, and mindfulness meditation. These techniques can help them cope with feelings of anxiety and manage their symptoms.

It is also important for parents and caregivers to provide emotional support and understanding for adolescents with anxiety disorders. They can help by listening to their concerns, validating their feelings, and providing reassurance when needed. This can help teenagers feel more comfortable and supported in seeking treatment for their anxiety.

Professional treatment can also be highly effective in helping adolescents manage their anxiety symptoms. Cognitive-behavioral therapy (CBT) is a common treatment approach for anxiety disorders and can be tailored to meet the unique needs of adolescents. CBT focuses on identifying and changing negative thought patterns and behaviors that contribute to anxiety symptoms. It can also teach coping strategies for managing anxiety in specific situations, such as academic or social stressors.

In some cases, medication may be prescribed to help manage anxiety symptoms. However, it is important to note that medication should always be used in conjunction with therapy and under the guidance of a mental health professional.

Preparing for the transition to adulthood

Anxiety disorders are one of the most common mental health issues faced by adolescents, affecting nearly one in three individuals. While anxiety is a normal and healthy response to stress, excessive and persistent anxiety can interfere with a young person's daily life, including their performance at school, their social relationships, and their overall well-being. For adolescents with anxiety disorders, the transition to adulthood can be particularly challenging.

As teenagers prepare to leave the nest, the world can seem like a much larger and more daunting place. Anxiety can intensify as adolescents face new challenges, such as going to college, moving away from home, and starting a new job. These challenges can be overwhelming, and it is important for parents, caregivers, and educators to understand how they can support adolescents with anxiety during this time.

One of the biggest challenges for adolescents with anxiety is navigating school. For many, school is a significant source of stress and anxiety, as they face pressures to perform academically, socially, and athletically. They may worry about fitting in, getting good grades, or impressing teachers and coaches. These worries can make it difficult to concentrate on schoolwork and may cause adolescents to avoid certain classes or activities altogether.

Parents and educators can support adolescents with anxiety by creating a safe and supportive environment. It is important to encourage open communication and to validate the teenager's concerns. Parents can help their children set realistic goals and provide them with the tools they need to succeed. Educators can provide accommodations, such as extra time on tests or assignments, and create a positive classroom environment that promotes inclusion and belonging.

Another challenge for adolescents with anxiety is maintaining social relationships. Adolescents with anxiety may struggle with social skills, making it difficult for them to form and maintain friendships. They may also be self-conscious and avoid social situations altogether, leading to feelings of loneliness and isolation.

Parents and caregivers can support adolescents with anxiety by helping them develop social skills and providing opportunities to practice them. This may include encouraging them to join clubs or extracurricular activities, volunteering, or participating in community events. It is also important to help adolescents with anxiety set boundaries and learn to say no to activities that may be overwhelming.

As adolescents prepare to transition to adulthood, they face new challenges related to independence and responsibility. For many, this involves going to college, moving away from home, and starting a new job. These changes can be particularly difficult for adolescents with anxiety, who may struggle with uncertainty and the fear of the unknown.

Parents and caregivers can support adolescents with anxiety by helping them develop coping strategies and problem-solving skills. It is important to encourage adolescents to take small steps towards independence and to provide them with opportunities to practice decision-making and problem-solving. This may include encouraging them to take on new responsibilities at home or in the community, or helping them develop a plan for the future.

Chapter Fifteen

Anxiety in the Workplace

Anxiety disorders are among the most common mental health conditions, affecting millions of individuals worldwide. These disorders can have a significant impact on a person's daily life, including their ability to perform their job effectively. Anxiety in the workplace is a common concern, as it can affect an individual's productivity, job satisfaction, and overall well-being. Below we will explore the impact of anxiety disorders on the workplace, including common triggers, symptoms, and strategies for managing anxiety in a professional setting.

Anxiety disorders can arise from a variety of causes, including genetic predisposition, environmental factors, and life experiences. In the workplace, certain triggers can exacerbate anxiety symptoms, such as excessive workload, job insecurity, social pressure, and conflict with colleagues or superiors. Individuals with anxiety disorders may also experience anticipatory anxiety, fearing upcoming work-related events, such as meetings, presentations, or evaluations.

The symptoms of anxiety can vary widely between individuals, but common signs include excessive worry, nervousness, restlessness, irritability, difficulty concentrating, and physical symptoms such as muscle tension, headaches, and gastrointestinal issues. These symptoms can significantly impact an individual's ability to perform their job duties, particularly those that require a high level of concentration, communication, or public speaking.

There are several strategies that individuals with anxiety disorders can use to manage their symptoms in the workplace. One of the most effective approaches is cognitive-behavioral therapy (CBT), a type of talk therapy that focuses on identifying and changing negative thought patterns and behaviors. CBT can help individuals develop coping skills and resilience to manage their anxiety in a professional setting.

In addition to therapy, individuals with anxiety disorders can also benefit from lifestyle modifications, such as exercise, adequate sleep, and a healthy diet. Regular exercise has been shown to reduce anxiety symptoms and improve overall mental health. Proper sleep hygiene can also help reduce anxiety symptoms, as sleep deprivation can exacerbate stress and anxiety.

Mindfulness meditation and relaxation techniques, such as deep breathing exercises and progressive muscle relaxation, can help individuals with anxiety disorders manage their symptoms in the workplace. These techniques can be used to reduce tension and promote relaxation during times of stress or anxiety.

It is important for individuals with anxiety disorders to communicate their needs and concerns with their employer or supervisor. Workplace accommodations, such as flexible scheduling or a reduced workload, can help individuals manage their symptoms and remain productive in their job. Additionally, supportive colleagues and a positive work environment can help reduce stress and anxiety in the workplace.

In some cases, medication may be prescribed to manage anxiety symptoms. Antidepressants, anti-anxiety medications, and beta-blockers are commonly prescribed for anxiety disorders. It is important to note that medication alone is not a cure for anxiety disorders and should be used in conjunction with therapy and lifestyle modifications.

Employers can also play a role in reducing workplace anxiety. Providing resources and support for employees with anxiety disorders, such as an employee assistance program or access to mental health professionals, can promote mental health and productivity in the workplace. Employers can also create a positive work environment by promoting work-life balance, offering employee recognition programs, and encouraging open communication between employees and supervisors.

Identifying work-related stressors

Work-related stress can be a significant contributor to anxiety disorders. Identifying the specific stressors that trigger anxiety can be an essential step in managing and overcoming anxiety in the workplace.

Common stressors in the workplace may include high workloads, long working hours, poor relationships with coworkers or managers, and lack of job security. Additionally, changes in job responsibilities, job loss, or significant organizational changes can also cause anxiety.

One way to identify work-related stressors is to monitor feelings and symptoms experienced during the workday. For example, if an individual experiences anxiety in the form of stomach aches or tension headaches, it may be helpful to keep a log of these symptoms and the context in which they occur. By identifying patterns in symptoms and linking them to specific situations, individuals may be able to identify work-related stressors and work to address them.

Another way to identify stressors is to seek feedback from coworkers or managers. For example, an individual may ask for feedback on their performance or ask a coworker for their perspective on how they manage their workload. This can help identify areas where improvements can be made to reduce anxiety-inducing situations.

It may also be helpful to evaluate the work environment itself, such as the physical space, work culture, and organizational policies. A poorly designed workspace, a toxic work culture, or policies that are not supportive of employee well-being can all contribute to work-related stress and anxiety.

Finally, seeking the assistance of a mental health professional can be beneficial in identifying work-related stressors. A therapist can help an individual explore the sources of their anxiety and provide strategies to manage and reduce anxiety in the workplace.

Identifying work-related stressors is an essential step in managing anxiety in the workplace. Through careful observation, seeking feedback, evaluating the work environment, and seeking professional help, individuals can better understand the sources of their anxiety and take action to manage it effectively.

Seeking accommodations and support

Anxiety disorders can have a significant impact on an individual's ability to perform well in the workplace. As such, seeking accommodations and support can be a crucial step towards managing anxiety symptoms and improving job performance. Below we will explore the different types of accommodations and support that may be available to those with anxiety disorders in the workplace.

One common accommodation that employers may provide is flexible work arrangements. This can include flexible hours, working from home, or reduced work hours. By allowing employees to work in a way that suits their needs and reduces stress, they may be better equipped to manage their anxiety symptoms. For example, if an employee experiences high levels of anxiety during peak traffic hours, a flexible work schedule may allow them to avoid these stressful situations altogether.

Another accommodation that employers may provide is a quiet workspace. This can be particularly beneficial for those with anxiety disorders, as it can reduce distractions and help individuals focus on their work. If a quiet workspace is not possible, noise-canceling headphones may also be an option.

Employers may also provide accommodations related to communication. For example, some individuals with anxiety disorders may find it difficult to communicate in group settings. By allowing them to communicate through email or providing regular one-on-one meetings, employers can help alleviate this anxiety and ensure that the individual feels heard and valued.

In addition to accommodations, support from coworkers and supervisors can also be beneficial. This can include being patient and understanding when an individual is experiencing anxiety symptoms, providing encouragement and positive feedback, and offering to assist with tasks that may be particularly challenging.

Employers may also provide resources such as an employee assistance program (EAP) or access to mental health professionals. These resources can provide employees with the tools and support they need to manage their anxiety symptoms, as well as help them identify triggers and coping strategies.

Finally, it is important for individuals with anxiety disorders to prioritize self-care and stress management techniques both in and outside of the workplace. This can include practicing mindfulness, engaging in regular exercise, getting enough sleep, and seeking social support.

Balancing work-life demands

Anxiety disorders can have a significant impact on an individual's ability to manage their work and personal life. For many people, work-related stressors can contribute to the development or exacerbation of anxiety symptoms. However, there are strategies that can be used to balance work-life demands and manage anxiety symptoms.

One of the first steps in balancing work-life demands is to identify potential stressors. Common work-related stressors include high workload, poor communication with coworkers or supervisors, job insecurity, and lack of control over one's work. Personal stressors may include family responsibilities, financial difficulties, or health issues. It's important to recognize that everyone's stressors are unique and that what may cause stress for one person may not cause stress for another.

Once stressors are identified, it may be helpful to seek accommodations and support from coworkers and supervisors. For example, if workload is a major stressor, it may be possible to delegate tasks or negotiate deadlines with a supervisor. Some employers may offer accommodations such as flexible scheduling, the option to work from home, or counseling services through an employee assistance program.

Self-care practices can also help manage work-related stressors and anxiety symptoms. This may include taking breaks throughout the workday to practice relaxation techniques, such as deep breathing or progressive muscle relaxation. Engaging in regular exercise, maintaining a healthy diet, and getting adequate sleep are also important components of self-care.

Another important aspect of balancing work-life demands is setting boundaries. It can be tempting to bring work home or to work during personal time, but this can ultimately lead to burnout and increased anxiety symptoms. Setting specific times for work and personal activities can help create a better balance and reduce stress.

Effective communication with coworkers and supervisors is also important in managing work-related stressors. This may involve setting clear expectations, expressing concerns, and asking for feedback. Establishing open lines of communication can help prevent misunderstandings and reduce anxiety related to work-related tasks and expectations.

Finally, it's important to recognize when additional support may be needed. This may include seeking help from a mental health professional, such as a therapist or psychiatrist, or joining a support group for individuals with anxiety disorders. Taking steps to address anxiety symptoms can help improve overall quality of life and enhance work performance.

Chapter Sixteen

Anxiety and Relationships

Anxiety can have a significant impact on relationships. Whether it's a romantic relationship, friendship, or family bond, anxiety can cause a range of challenges and difficulties that can impact the relationship's quality and longevity. It's essential to recognize the signs of anxiety and understand how it can affect relationships to develop healthy and supportive relationships that can withstand the challenges of anxiety.

One of the most significant ways anxiety can impact relationships is by creating tension and conflict. Anxiety can cause individuals to become easily overwhelmed and irritable, leading to arguments and misunderstandings. Anxiety can also cause individuals to become overly critical or defensive, making it difficult to communicate effectively and navigate challenges. It's essential to recognize when anxiety is impacting your interactions with others and work to address the underlying causes of the anxiety to improve communication and reduce conflict.

Anxiety can also lead individuals to withdraw from relationships. When individuals experience anxiety, they may avoid social situations, cancel plans, or become disengaged from their relationships, which can lead to feelings of isolation and loneliness. It's essential to communicate with your loved ones and express your feelings and concerns. If you're experiencing anxiety, it's essential to communicate your needs and work together to find ways to support your mental health while maintaining your relationships.

Anxiety can also impact intimacy and sexual relationships. Individuals with anxiety may experience sexual dysfunction, decreased libido, or difficulty connecting with their partners on an emotional level. Anxiety can cause individuals to become self-conscious or experience feelings of inadequacy, making it challenging to be vulnerable with their partners. It's essential to communicate openly and honestly with your partner and seek professional help if necessary to address any underlying issues related to anxiety and sexual health.

If you or your partner experience anxiety, it's important to seek support and develop healthy coping strategies. This may involve therapy, medication, or self-care practices such as mindfulness, exercise, or journaling. It's also essential to communicate your needs and boundaries in your relationships and work together to create a supportive and understanding environment. Building a strong support system and prioritizing your mental health can help you manage anxiety and develop healthy and fulfilling relationships.

Anxiety can impact relationships in a range of ways, but it doesn't have to define them. By recognizing the signs of anxiety and working to address its underlying causes, individuals can develop healthy and supportive relationships that can withstand the challenges of anxiety. It's essential to communicate openly and honestly, prioritize mental health, and seek professional support when necessary to develop relationships that promote health and happiness.

The impact of anxiety on romantic partnerships and friendships

Anxiety can have a significant impact on both romantic partnerships and friendships. When an individual experiences anxiety, they may struggle with trust issues, feel overwhelmed by social situations, and have difficulty managing their emotions. These struggles can make it challenging to maintain healthy relationships.

In romantic partnerships, anxiety can cause a range of issues. For example, an individual with anxiety may struggle with trust issues, leading them to constantly question their partner's loyalty or faithfulness. They may also struggle with feelings of jealousy and insecurity, which can create tension in the relationship.

Anxiety can also cause an individual to withdraw emotionally, making it difficult to connect with their partner on a deeper level. This emotional distance can create feelings of loneliness and isolation for both partners.

In friendships, anxiety can cause similar issues. An individual with anxiety may struggle with social situations, making it difficult to attend events or engage in activities with friends. This social withdrawal can lead to feelings of isolation and disconnection, making it challenging to maintain close friendships.

Additionally, anxiety can cause an individual to struggle with communication, making it challenging to express their needs and feelings effectively. This lack of communication can lead to misunderstandings and conflict within the friendship.

Despite the challenges that anxiety can pose in relationships, there are ways to manage these struggles and maintain healthy connections with others.

One important step is to seek treatment for anxiety. By addressing the underlying anxiety disorder, an individual can learn coping skills and strategies to manage their symptoms. This can make it easier to build and maintain healthy relationships.

It's also important to communicate openly and honestly with romantic partners and friends. This may involve sharing your struggles with anxiety and how it affects your relationships. By being open and vulnerable, you can foster deeper connections and build trust with those around you.

In romantic partnerships, couples can work together to establish trust and boundaries. For example, couples can agree to check in with each other regularly or establish guidelines for spending time with friends of the opposite sex.

In friendships, it's important to be patient and understanding. Recognize that your friend may be struggling with anxiety and may need additional support and patience during difficult times. Encourage your friend to seek treatment and offer to help them connect with resources if needed.

Finally, taking care of yourself is an important aspect of maintaining healthy relationships when you have anxiety. This may involve practicing self-care activities like exercise, mindfulness, and healthy eating. By prioritizing your own well-being, you can reduce the impact of anxiety on your relationships and maintain healthy connections with those around you.

Communication strategies for healthy connections

Anxiety can have a significant impact on our relationships with others. It can cause difficulties in communication, lead to avoidance behaviors, and create feelings of insecurity and isolation. Therefore, it is essential to develop effective communication strategies to maintain healthy connections with others despite experiencing anxiety.

The first step to building healthy relationships while managing anxiety is to become aware of how anxiety manifests in ourselves. Anxiety can cause physical symptoms such as racing heart, sweating, and trembling, as well as mental symptoms such as racing thoughts and irrational fears. Understanding our own anxiety symptoms can help us communicate more effectively with our loved ones about what we need from them when we are feeling anxious.

It is also important to practice self-care when experiencing anxiety in relationships. This can involve taking breaks when feeling overwhelmed, engaging in relaxation techniques, and seeking professional support when necessary. Self-care is not only essential for managing anxiety but also for building healthy relationships, as it allows us to show up fully present and engaged with our loved ones.

Another crucial aspect of effective communication in relationships is learning how to express our feelings and needs in a clear and assertive manner. Anxiety can often lead to passive or aggressive communication styles, which can be damaging to relationships. Learning to express ourselves assertively while still being mindful of others' feelings and needs can help build healthy communication patterns and foster understanding and trust in our relationships.

Moreover, it is important to actively listen to our loved ones when they express their feelings and needs. Active listening involves paying attention to what the other person is saying, reflecting on their words, and responding thoughtfully. It is not about providing solutions or advice but rather about creating a safe and supportive space for our loved ones to share their experiences.

In addition to improving communication skills, it is also helpful to create boundaries in our relationships to manage anxiety. Boundaries involve setting limits on what we are willing and able to do and communicating those limits to our loved ones. This can include saying no to social events that are triggering, asking for space when feeling overwhelmed, or communicating our needs around touch or physical proximity.

Finally, it is important to remember that relationships are a two-way street. While it is essential to develop effective communication strategies and practice self-care to manage anxiety in relationships, it is also crucial for our loved ones to be supportive and understanding of our needs. If a relationship is causing significant distress or is not supportive of our mental health needs, it may be necessary to re-evaluate that relationship and seek support from others.

Building and maintaining a supportive network

Building and maintaining a supportive network for individuals with anxiety disorders is crucial in promoting their overall well-being and quality of life. A support system can provide emotional and practical support, offer encouragement and motivation, and help individuals with anxiety disorders feel less alone in their struggles. Below we will discuss the importance of building a supportive network and offer tips on how to create and maintain one.

One of the most significant challenges for people with anxiety disorders is feeling isolated and misunderstood. They may feel ashamed or embarrassed about their symptoms, making it challenging to open up to others. A supportive network can help individuals with anxiety disorders feel heard and understood, reduce feelings of shame and stigma, and promote a sense of belonging and connection.

A supportive network can consist of friends, family members, mental health professionals, support groups, and online communities. It is essential to build a network of people who understand and support your struggles with anxiety. Having people who are willing to listen and provide practical and emotional support can make a significant difference in your ability to manage your symptoms.

When building a support network, it is essential to reach out to people you trust and feel comfortable talking to about your anxiety. This may include close friends or family members, a therapist, or a support group. Try to identify individuals who are compassionate, empathetic, and non-judgmental.

It is also essential to educate those in your support system about your anxiety disorder. Provide information about your symptoms, triggers, and coping strategies. This can help them better understand what you are going through and offer more effective support.

Communication is key to building and maintaining a supportive network. It is essential to be open and honest with those in your support system about your feelings and needs. It may be helpful to establish clear communication channels, such as regular check-ins or scheduled conversations, to ensure that you stay connected.

Participating in support groups or online communities can also be helpful in building a supportive network. These groups offer a safe and supportive space to connect with others who are experiencing similar challenges. They provide an opportunity to share experiences, learn coping strategies, and offer support and encouragement.

It is also essential to maintain healthy boundaries when building a support network. It is essential to be clear about your needs and expectations for support while also respecting the needs and boundaries of others. Remember that support is a two-way street, and it is crucial to offer support to those in your network when they need it.

Another essential aspect of building and maintaining a supportive network is self-care. It is crucial to prioritize your own well-being and engage in activities that promote relaxation, stress reduction, and overall health. This can include exercise, mindfulness practices, hobbies, or spending time with loved ones.

Chapter Seventeen

Women and Anxiety

Anxiety is a common mental health disorder that affects millions of people worldwide. Studies have shown that women are more likely to experience anxiety than men, with about 1 in 5 women experiencing anxiety at some point in their lives. Below we will explore the reasons why women are more susceptible to anxiety and the impact it can have on their lives.

There are several factors that contribute to the higher incidence of anxiety in women. Hormonal fluctuations, especially during menstruation, pregnancy, and menopause, have been linked to increased anxiety levels. Women are also more likely to experience traumatic events, such as sexual assault or domestic violence, which can lead to anxiety and other mental health disorders.

Societal expectations and gender roles also play a significant role in women's anxiety. Women are often expected to juggle multiple responsibilities, including work, home, and caregiving, leading to high levels of stress and anxiety. The pressure to conform to unrealistic beauty standards and societal expectations of perfection can also contribute to anxiety and low self-esteem.

The impact of anxiety on women's lives can be significant, affecting their physical health, relationships, and work productivity. Anxiety can cause physical symptoms such as chest pain, headaches, and difficulty breathing, which can impact daily activities and cause further stress. Women with anxiety are also more likely to have difficulties with relationships, including increased conflict and decreased satisfaction. Anxiety can also lead to decreased work productivity, absenteeism, and job loss, which can have long-term economic consequences.

Fortunately, there are several strategies that women can use to manage anxiety and improve their overall well-being. Cognitive-behavioral therapy (CBT) is an evidence-based treatment that can help women identify and challenge negative thought patterns and develop coping skills to manage anxiety. Mindfulness meditation and relaxation techniques have also been shown to be effective in reducing anxiety symptoms. Exercise, a healthy diet, and adequate sleep can also help improve overall physical and mental health.

Building a supportive network is also crucial for managing anxiety. Women can benefit from connecting with others who have similar experiences, such as joining a support group or seeking therapy. Building positive relationships with family and friends can also provide emotional support and help reduce feelings of isolation and anxiety.

In addition, self-care practices such as taking breaks, setting boundaries, and prioritizing self-care can help women manage stress and reduce anxiety levels. This can include engaging in hobbies, practicing gratitude, and engaging in activities that bring joy and fulfillment.

The unique experiences of women with anxiety disorders

Anxiety disorders are a common mental health issue that affects millions of people worldwide. Among those who suffer from anxiety disorders, women are more likely to experience them than men. Anxiety can be triggered by various factors, including environmental, social, and biological factors, and women may be more susceptible to these triggers due to the unique experiences they face.

Women experience anxiety disorders at twice the rate of men, and this difference is thought to be due to a combination of factors. Women are more likely to experience trauma, including sexual abuse and assault, which can contribute to the development of anxiety disorders. Women may also experience higher levels of stress due to societal expectations, such as caring for children and managing a household, which can be overwhelming and lead to anxiety.

Women's hormonal fluctuations may also contribute to anxiety. The menstrual cycle, pregnancy, and menopause are all periods when hormones fluctuate and may lead to increased anxiety levels. Additionally, women may be more likely to experience anxiety during times of hormonal changes due to stress and lack of sleep.

Anxiety disorders can also be impacted by the social and cultural roles that women are expected to play. Women are often expected to be nurturing and caring, and this can lead to feelings of guilt and shame when they are unable to meet these expectations. The pressure to balance work, family, and social responsibilities can be overwhelming, leading to anxiety.

Furthermore, women may be more likely to internalize their anxiety, leading to feelings of isolation and shame. They may also be more likely to seek help from friends and family rather than seeking professional treatment. However, seeking professional help can be critical in managing anxiety disorders.

Women may also experience different types of anxiety disorders than men. For example, women are more likely to experience generalized anxiety disorder, panic disorder, and social anxiety disorder. Generalized anxiety disorder is characterized by excessive and persistent worry about everyday events, while panic disorder involves sudden and unexpected panic attacks. Social anxiety disorder involves intense fear and anxiety in social situations, and women are more likely to experience this disorder than men.

Fortunately, there are effective treatments for anxiety disorders that women can pursue. Therapy, particularly cognitive-behavioral therapy (CBT), is an evidence-based treatment that helps people identify and challenge negative thought patterns and behaviors that contribute to anxiety. Medications, such as selective serotonin reuptake inhibitors (SSRIs), can also be effective in managing anxiety symptoms.

Additionally, self-care strategies can be beneficial in managing anxiety. Regular exercise, healthy eating habits, and getting enough sleep can all help to reduce anxiety symptoms. Mindfulness and relaxation techniques, such as meditation and yoga, can also be beneficial in managing anxiety.

Hormonal influences and life transitions

Anxiety is a common mental health condition that affects people of all ages and genders. However, studies have shown that women are more likely to experience anxiety than men. Women may experience anxiety symptoms in different ways than men, and hormonal changes throughout a woman's life can impact anxiety levels. Understanding the unique experiences of women with anxiety can help promote effective treatment and management strategies.

Hormonal influences are one of the factors that contribute to the unique experiences of women with anxiety. Hormones such as estrogen and progesterone can affect neurotransmitters in the brain, such as serotonin and dopamine, which play a role in regulating mood and anxiety. Fluctuations in hormone levels can cause changes in these neurotransmitters and result in anxiety symptoms.

Women may experience anxiety symptoms at different points in their hormonal cycles. For example, premenstrual syndrome (PMS) is a common condition experienced by many women, and it can cause symptoms such as anxiety, irritability, and mood swings in the days leading up to a woman's period. Postpartum depression and anxiety are also common among new mothers, and the hormonal changes that occur during pregnancy and childbirth can impact a woman's mental health.

Life transitions such as menopause can also impact anxiety levels in women. As women age, their estrogen levels decrease, which can lead to changes in mood and anxiety levels. Additionally, menopause can be a stressful time for women as they navigate physical and emotional changes. The combination of hormonal fluctuations and life stressors can make women more vulnerable to anxiety during this time.

The unique experiences of women with anxiety extend beyond hormonal influences. Women may also face gender-specific stressors that contribute to anxiety levels. For example, women may be more likely to experience sexual harassment or assault, which can lead to feelings of anxiety, fear, and helplessness. Additionally, women may face societal pressure to meet certain standards of appearance and behavior, which can contribute to feelings of anxiety and low self-esteem.

Women may also experience anxiety symptoms in different ways than men. Women may be more likely to experience physical symptoms of anxiety, such as heart palpitations, dizziness, and nausea. Women may also be more likely to experience social anxiety, which is characterized by a fear of social situations and performance anxiety.

Effective treatment and management strategies for women with anxiety should take into account these unique experiences. Treatment options such as cognitive-behavioral therapy (CBT) and medication can be effective for both men and women with anxiety, but may need to be tailored to address specific concerns and stressors faced by women. Hormonal therapies such as birth control pills or hormone replacement therapy may also be effective for women whose anxiety is impacted by hormonal fluctuations.

Self-care strategies such as regular exercise, healthy eating, and stress management techniques can be beneficial for all people with anxiety, but may be especially important for women experiencing hormonal changes. Support groups and therapy can also provide a space for women to connect with others and share their experiences.

Treatment considerations for women

Anxiety disorders affect people of all genders and ages, but they can manifest differently in women due to unique hormonal influences and life transitions. While treatment options for anxiety disorders are generally the same regardless of gender, it is important to take into account the specific needs and considerations of women when developing a treatment plan.

One factor to consider is hormonal influences. Women experience hormonal changes throughout their lives, particularly during puberty, menstruation, pregnancy, and menopause. These changes can trigger or exacerbate anxiety symptoms. For example, premenstrual dysphoric disorder (PMDD) is a condition that affects some women during the days leading up to their period and can cause intense mood swings, irritability, and anxiety.

Hormonal birth control can also affect anxiety symptoms. Some women report increased anxiety while taking hormonal birth control, while others report a decrease in symptoms. It is important for women to discuss their hormonal status and any medications they are taking with their healthcare provider to determine if these factors may be contributing to their anxiety.

In addition to hormonal influences, life transitions can also impact anxiety symptoms in women. Women may experience anxiety related to parenting, caregiving, career changes, and relationship issues. For example, new mothers may experience postpartum anxiety or depression, which can be characterized by excessive worry about the baby's health and safety.

When developing a treatment plan for women with anxiety, it is important to consider these unique factors. Cognitive-behavioral therapy (CBT) is a common treatment option for anxiety disorders and can be particularly effective for women. CBT focuses on changing negative thought patterns and developing healthy coping strategies.

In addition to therapy, medication may also be an option for women with anxiety disorders. However, some medications may not be suitable for women who are pregnant or breastfeeding, so it is important for women to discuss their medication options with their healthcare provider.

Self-care practices can also be helpful for women with anxiety. Regular exercise, healthy eating, and getting enough sleep can all help manage anxiety symptoms. Mindfulness practices such as meditation and deep breathing exercises can also be beneficial.

Women may also benefit from joining support groups or seeking out other forms of social support. Connecting with other women who have experienced similar struggles can help women feel less alone and provide them with practical advice for managing their symptoms.

It is important to note that women may face unique barriers to accessing treatment for anxiety disorders. Stigma surrounding mental health and gender-based discrimination can prevent women from seeking the help they need. It is important for healthcare providers to be aware of these barriers and work to create a safe and supportive environment for women seeking treatment.

Chapter Eighteen

Men and Anxiety

Anxiety is a common mental health condition that affects individuals regardless of gender. However, research has found that men are less likely to seek treatment for anxiety than women. Men may feel societal pressure to conceal their emotions and appear strong, which can make it challenging to recognize and seek help for anxiety.

The symptoms of anxiety in men can vary but may include feelings of restlessness or irritability, difficulty sleeping, muscle tension, and avoidance of certain situations. Anxiety can also co-occur with other mental health conditions such as depression or substance abuse.

One unique factor that can contribute to anxiety in men is the pressure to conform to traditional gender roles. Men may feel pressure to be the breadwinner or to appear strong and in control at all times. These societal expectations can lead to feelings of inadequacy or failure when they are not met, which can contribute to anxiety.

It is essential for men to seek treatment for anxiety to improve their overall mental health and wellbeing. Treatment options for anxiety can include therapy, medication, and lifestyle changes. Therapy can be particularly beneficial for men as it provides a safe space to explore their thoughts and emotions and develop healthy coping mechanisms. Cognitive-behavioral therapy (CBT) is a common therapy approach for anxiety and can help individuals recognize and challenge negative thought patterns.

Medications such as antidepressants and anti-anxiety medications can also be effective in managing anxiety symptoms. However, it is important to note that medications should be prescribed and monitored by a healthcare professional.

Lifestyle changes can also be helpful in managing anxiety symptoms. Regular exercise, a healthy diet, and stress-reducing activities such as meditation or yoga can all contribute to improved mental health.

Men may also benefit from seeking support from friends and family or joining a support group for individuals with anxiety. Building a supportive network can provide a sense of community and help individuals feel less alone in their struggles with anxiety.

Recognizing anxiety symptoms in men

Anxiety is a common mental health condition that affects people of all genders, including men. Unfortunately, many men may not recognize the symptoms of anxiety or may feel reluctant to seek help due to social stigma and pressure to appear strong and in control. It is crucial to raise awareness about the signs of anxiety in men so that they can receive the support and treatment they need.

The symptoms of anxiety in men may vary, but some common signs include restlessness, irritability, trouble sleeping, fatigue, muscle tension, and excessive worrying. Men with anxiety may also experience physical symptoms such as chest pain, headaches, digestive problems, and sweating. It is important to note that these symptoms can also indicate other health conditions, so it is essential to consult a healthcare professional for a proper diagnosis.

One reason men may be less likely to recognize anxiety symptoms is that they may experience anxiety differently than women. Men may be more likely to express their anxiety through physical symptoms or behaviors rather than talking about their feelings. For example, some men may turn to alcohol or drugs to cope with anxiety, engage in risky behaviors, or become overly controlling or aggressive in relationships.

Another reason men may hesitate to seek help for anxiety is societal expectations of masculinity. Men may feel pressure to appear strong and self-sufficient and may fear being perceived as weak or vulnerable if they seek help for anxiety. It is essential to challenge these harmful stereotypes and promote a more open and accepting culture around mental health.

Fortunately, there are effective treatments available for anxiety that can help men manage their symptoms and improve their quality of life. Treatment options may include therapy, medication, or a combination of both. Cognitive-behavioral therapy (CBT) is a type of talk therapy that can help individuals identify and challenge negative thought patterns and develop healthy coping skills. Medications such as antidepressants or anti-anxiety medications can also be helpful for managing anxiety symptoms.

In addition to professional treatment, there are also self-help strategies that men can use to manage their anxiety. Regular exercise, healthy eating, and getting enough sleep can all help to reduce stress and improve mood. Engaging in hobbies and activities that bring joy and fulfillment can also be beneficial for managing anxiety. Mindfulness practices such as meditation, deep breathing, and yoga can also help to calm the mind and reduce anxiety symptoms.

Support from loved ones can also be invaluable for men with anxiety. Building a supportive network of friends and family members who understand and accept their struggles can provide a sense of validation and reduce feelings of isolation. Men may also find it helpful to join a support group or seek out online communities of people who share similar experiences.

Addressing stigma and barriers to treatment

Addressing Stigma and Barriers to Treatment for Anxiety Disorders

Anxiety disorders are among the most common mental health conditions worldwide, affecting people of all ages, genders, and backgrounds. Despite the prevalence of anxiety disorders, many individuals who suffer from these conditions do not receive appropriate treatment due to various barriers, including stigma, lack of awareness, financial constraints, and inadequate access to care. Below we will explore the impact of stigma and other barriers to treatment for anxiety disorders, as well as strategies for addressing these obstacles to improve outcomes for those who are affected.

Stigma is a major barrier to seeking and receiving treatment for anxiety disorders. Stigma refers to negative attitudes and beliefs about mental illness, which can lead to social rejection, discrimination, and even self-stigma. Stigma can be a significant obstacle to treatment because it prevents individuals from seeking help, either because they fear being labeled as "crazy" or "weak," or because they believe that their anxiety is a personal weakness rather than a medical condition. Stigma can also lead to underdiagnosis and undertreatment of anxiety disorders, as healthcare providers may be less likely to recognize and treat these conditions due to a lack of training or negative stereotypes about mental illness.

Another significant barrier to treatment for anxiety disorders is lack of awareness. Many people may not be aware that they are experiencing symptoms of an anxiety disorder, or may mistake their symptoms for a physical ailment or normal stress. Additionally, many individuals may not be aware of the treatment options available for anxiety disorders, or may not know where to seek care. This lack of awareness can lead to delays in seeking treatment and can worsen the severity of symptoms over time.

Financial constraints can also prevent individuals from seeking and receiving treatment for anxiety disorders. The cost of treatment can be a significant barrier, particularly for those without health insurance or those whose insurance does not cover mental health services. In some cases, the cost of treatment may be prohibitive even for those with insurance, as co-pays and deductibles can add up quickly. This financial burden can lead to delayed or inadequate treatment, as individuals may be unable to afford the medications, therapy, or other interventions needed to manage their symptoms.

Inadequate access to care is another barrier to treatment for anxiety disorders. Many individuals who seek treatment for anxiety disorders face long wait times for appointments, limited availability of mental health professionals, and difficulty accessing care in rural or low-income areas. Additionally, some individuals may face language or cultural barriers that prevent them from accessing appropriate care. These access barriers can result in delayed or inadequate treatment, leading to more severe symptoms and decreased quality of life.

To address the barriers to treatment for anxiety disorders, several strategies can be implemented. These strategies include:

Increasing awareness and education about anxiety disorders and their treatment options. Public education campaigns and targeted outreach efforts can help individuals better understand the symptoms and impact of anxiety disorders, as well as the available treatment options.

Addressing stigma and negative attitudes towards mental illness through anti-stigma campaigns and education programs. This can help reduce the shame and embarrassment associated with seeking treatment for anxiety disorders and encourage individuals to seek help when needed.

Improving access to care by increasing the availability of mental health professionals and services in underserved areas, and promoting the use of telemedicine and other remote healthcare technologies to improve access to care for those in rural or remote areas.

Providing financial assistance to individuals who cannot afford treatment for anxiety disorders, such as through government programs or sliding scale fees for mental health services.

Encouraging healthcare providers to screen for anxiety disorders and provide evidence-based treatments to those who need it. This can include training programs for healthcare providers on the diagnosis and treatment of anxiety disorders, as well as the importance of early intervention and ongoing care.

Cultivating emotional intelligence and self-awareness

Cultivating emotional intelligence and self-awareness can be an effective way to manage anxiety disorders. Emotional intelligence is the ability to identify, understand, and manage emotions in oneself and others. Self-awareness is the ability to recognize one's own emotions and how they affect thoughts and behaviors. Both skills can help individuals with anxiety disorders to recognize and regulate their emotions, which can reduce the severity and frequency of anxiety symptoms.

Emotional intelligence and self-awareness can be developed through a variety of techniques, including mindfulness meditation, journaling, and therapy. Mindfulness meditation involves focusing attention on the present moment, without judgment, and accepting one's thoughts and feelings. This can help individuals with anxiety disorders to observe their thoughts and emotions without becoming overwhelmed by them. Journaling can also be helpful in developing emotional intelligence and self-awareness by providing a space to reflect on one's thoughts and feelings. Therapy can provide a supportive and non-judgmental environment to explore and understand one's emotions.

Developing emotional intelligence and self-awareness can also involve learning to recognize and label emotions. This can be especially important for individuals with anxiety disorders, who may struggle with identifying and expressing their emotions. Learning to recognize and label emotions can help individuals with anxiety disorders to identify triggers for their anxiety, as well as recognize when they are experiencing heightened anxiety symptoms.

Another important aspect of cultivating emotional intelligence and self-awareness is learning to regulate emotions. This involves developing skills to manage strong emotions, such as anxiety or panic. Techniques for regulating emotions can include deep breathing exercises, progressive muscle relaxation, and cognitive-behavioral therapy. Deep breathing exercises involve taking slow, deep breaths to calm the body and mind. Progressive muscle relaxation involves tensing and relaxing different muscle groups to reduce physical tension and anxiety. Cognitive-behavioral therapy is a form of therapy that focuses on changing negative thought patterns and behaviors that can contribute to anxiety.

In addition to these techniques, self-care can also be an important aspect of developing emotional intelligence and self-awareness. This can involve engaging in activities that promote well-being and reduce stress, such as exercise, spending time in nature, or practicing a hobby. Self-care can also involve setting boundaries and saying no to activities or relationships that are not beneficial to one's emotional health.

Chapter Nineteen

Aging and Anxiety

Anxiety is a common mental health concern that affects people of all ages, including older adults. As people age, they face a variety of physical and emotional changes that can contribute to anxiety. It's important for older adults, their families, and healthcare providers to be aware of the unique challenges and considerations associated with anxiety in later life.

One of the primary causes of anxiety in older adults is the experience of multiple losses. As people age, they may face the loss of loved ones, friends, and community members. They may also experience a decline in physical health, cognitive abilities, and independence. These losses can lead to feelings of grief, loneliness, and uncertainty about the future.

Other factors that can contribute to anxiety in older adults include social isolation, financial concerns, and health-related worries. Older adults may also be more vulnerable to the effects of stress due to age-related changes in the body's stress response system. These changes can make it more difficult for older adults to manage stress and cope with the demands of daily life.

It's important for older adults to receive appropriate treatment for anxiety, as it can have a negative impact on their physical health, social relationships, and quality of life. However, there are some unique considerations to keep in mind when treating anxiety in older adults.

First, it's important to recognize that older adults may be hesitant to seek treatment for anxiety due to the stigma surrounding mental health concerns. Healthcare providers should take the time to educate older adults and their families about the importance of seeking treatment for anxiety and the effective treatments available.

Second, healthcare providers should be aware of the potential for medication interactions in older adults. Many older adults take multiple medications to manage chronic health conditions, and some medications can interact with anti-anxiety medications. Healthcare providers should carefully monitor older adults who are taking anti-anxiety medications and adjust their medication regimen as needed.

Finally, it's important to recognize that older adults may have unique preferences and needs when it comes to treatment for anxiety. Some older adults may prefer non-medication approaches, such as therapy or relaxation techniques. Healthcare providers should work with older adults to develop a personalized treatment plan that takes into account their unique needs and preferences.

In addition to seeking appropriate treatment, there are some strategies that older adults can use to manage anxiety on their own. For example, staying physically active can help to reduce anxiety and improve overall physical and mental health. Older adults can also benefit from engaging in activities that promote social connection and a sense of purpose, such as volunteering or joining a social group.

Another important strategy for managing anxiety in older adults is to prioritize self-care. This may involve engaging in activities that promote relaxation and stress reduction, such as meditation, yoga, or tai chi. It may also involve taking steps to improve sleep quality, such as establishing a consistent bedtime routine and avoiding caffeine and alcohol before bed.

Anxiety disorders in older adults

Anxiety disorders are the most common mental health disorders among older adults, affecting up to 20% of this population. Anxiety disorders in older adults can be particularly challenging, as they can be overlooked or misdiagnosed due to the belief that anxiety is a natural part of aging. However, anxiety disorders can significantly impact quality of life and functioning in older adults, making it important to recognize and address them.

Some of the most common anxiety disorders in older adults include generalized anxiety disorder (GAD), panic disorder, and social anxiety disorder. These disorders can cause symptoms such as excessive worry, fear, and avoidance of certain situations. Physical symptoms can also occur, such as muscle tension, fatigue, and sleep disturbances.

There are several factors that can contribute to anxiety disorders in older adults, including changes in health and mobility, retirement, financial concerns, and social isolation. Older adults may also be more vulnerable to stressors such as chronic illness and loss of loved ones. Additionally, cognitive changes associated with aging, such as decreased memory and concentration, can exacerbate anxiety symptoms.

Diagnosing anxiety disorders in older adults can be challenging, as symptoms can be attributed to physical health problems or normal age-related changes. It is important for healthcare providers to conduct a thorough evaluation to rule out other potential causes of symptoms. Treatment for anxiety disorders in older adults can include medication, therapy, and lifestyle changes.

Medications such as selective serotonin reuptake inhibitors (SSRIs) and benzodiazepines can be effective in reducing anxiety symptoms. However, older adults may be more susceptible to side effects and medication interactions, making it important for healthcare providers to carefully monitor and adjust medication regimens.

Psychotherapy, particularly cognitive behavioral therapy (CBT), can be effective in treating anxiety disorders in older adults. CBT can help individuals identify and challenge negative thought patterns and learn coping skills to manage anxiety symptoms. Group therapy can also be helpful, as it provides opportunities for social support and skill-building.

Lifestyle changes can also be effective in managing anxiety symptoms in older adults. Regular exercise has been shown to reduce anxiety and improve overall well-being. Additionally, activities such as meditation and deep breathing exercises can help reduce stress and promote relaxation.

Support from family and friends is also important in managing anxiety disorders in older adults. Social support can provide a sense of connection and belonging, and can also help older adults cope with stress and anxiety. Healthcare providers can also refer older adults to support groups or community resources.

Navigating age-related challenges and changes

As we age, we face many changes and challenges that can impact our mental health, including anxiety. Anxiety disorders in older adults are common, yet they are often underdiagnosed and undertreated. Below we will explore some of the age-related challenges and changes that can lead to anxiety in older adults, as well as strategies for navigating these challenges.

One of the most significant age-related changes that can impact our mental health is the decline in physical health. As we age, we may develop chronic conditions such as arthritis, diabetes, or heart disease. These conditions can cause pain, discomfort, and limitations in mobility, which can lead to feelings of anxiety and depression. Additionally, older adults may have to adjust to a loss of independence, which can be a major source of anxiety.

Another age-related challenge that can contribute to anxiety is social isolation. As we age, we may lose touch with friends and family members or experience the loss of a spouse or partner. This can lead to feelings of loneliness and isolation, which can increase the risk of anxiety and depression. Additionally, older adults may experience ageism or discrimination, which can further exacerbate feelings of social isolation and anxiety.

The cognitive changes that occur with aging can also contribute to anxiety. As we get older, we may experience changes in memory and cognitive function, which can lead to feelings of uncertainty and confusion. This can be especially challenging for older adults who may have to navigate complex medical treatments or financial decisions.

Despite these challenges, there are many strategies that older adults can use to manage anxiety and maintain good mental health. One of the most important strategies is to stay connected with others. This can include maintaining relationships with friends and family members, joining a community group or social club, or volunteering. By staying connected with others, older adults can reduce feelings of social isolation and loneliness, which can help to prevent anxiety and depression.

Another strategy for managing anxiety in older adults is to engage in regular physical activity. Exercise has been shown to be an effective treatment for anxiety and depression, and it can also improve overall physical health. Even simple activities such as walking or stretching can have a positive impact on mental health.

It is also important for older adults to stay engaged in activities that bring them joy and fulfillment. This can include hobbies, travel, or volunteering.

By staying engaged in meaningful activities, older adults can maintain a sense of purpose and fulfillment, which can help to prevent feelings of anxiety and depression.

In addition to these strategies, older adults can also benefit from seeking professional help for anxiety. There are many effective treatments for anxiety, including talk therapy, medication, and relaxation techniques. By working with a mental health professional, older adults can learn new coping strategies and develop a personalized treatment plan that meets their unique needs.

Treatment considerations for the aging population

As individuals age, they may experience an increase in anxiety and worry due to a variety of factors, such as health concerns, retirement, or loss of loved ones. In fact, anxiety disorders are among the most common mental health concerns among older adults. While it is important to recognize and address anxiety in the aging population, there are unique treatment considerations to keep in mind.

One key consideration is the potential impact of other health conditions and medications. Many older adults have multiple chronic health conditions that can impact their physical and mental well-being, such as arthritis, diabetes, and heart disease. In addition, they may be taking multiple medications for these conditions, which can interact with each other and affect cognitive and emotional functioning. It is important for healthcare providers to carefully evaluate any potential interactions between anxiety medications and other medications an older adult may be taking. Additionally, they may need to monitor for side effects and adjust dosage accordingly.

Another consideration is the potential impact of cognitive decline on treatment effectiveness. As individuals age, they may experience cognitive changes that can impact their ability to engage in certain therapies, such as cognitive-behavioral therapy. This may require modifications to therapy techniques, such as simplifying instructions or incorporating more visual aids. Additionally, it may be important to include family members or caregivers in therapy sessions to provide support and help with treatment adherence.

Social isolation and loneliness are also common concerns among older adults, which can exacerbate anxiety symptoms. Healthcare providers may need to address these concerns by providing resources for social engagement, such as support groups or volunteer opportunities. Additionally, telehealth options may be beneficial for older adults who may have difficulty traveling to appointments.

Finally, it is important to consider the potential impact of ageism and stigma on seeking treatment for anxiety. Older adults may be more likely to view anxiety as a normal part of aging or may feel embarrassed or ashamed to seek help for mental health concerns. Healthcare providers can help address these concerns by providing education on the prevalence and treatability of anxiety disorders, as well as by normalizing seeking help for mental health concerns.

In terms of treatment options, there are several evidence-based interventions that have been found to be effective for treating anxiety in older adults. Cognitive-behavioral therapy (CBT) has been found to be effective for treating generalized anxiety disorder and panic disorder in older adults, with modifications to account for cognitive and physical changes associated with aging. Additionally, relaxation techniques such as progressive muscle relaxation and deep breathing exercises can be effective for reducing anxiety symptoms.

Pharmacotherapy, such as selective serotonin reuptake inhibitors (SSRIs), can also be effective for treating anxiety in older adults, but healthcare providers need to be cautious with dosage and potential interactions with other medications. Benzodiazepines are generally not recommended for older adults due to their potential for cognitive side effects and increased risk of falls.

Chapter Twenty

Anxiety and Technology

Anxiety disorders are a common mental health condition that can be caused by a variety of factors, including genetics, environment, and life experiences. With the rise of technology and social media, there has been an increased interest in how these factors impact mental health, including anxiety. Below we will explore the relationship between anxiety and technology and discuss some strategies for managing anxiety in a tech-driven world.

The Impact of Technology on Anxiety

Technology has dramatically changed the way we communicate, work, and live our lives. While technology has many benefits, it can also contribute to anxiety in several ways. For example, constant connectivity can lead to feelings of overwhelm and burnout. Social media can lead to feelings of isolation, comparison, and self-doubt. Excessive screen time can disrupt sleep, which can exacerbate anxiety symptoms.

Another way technology can impact anxiety is through information overload. With the constant stream of news and information available online, it can be challenging to filter out the noise and focus on what's important. This can lead to feelings of anxiety and uncertainty, especially during times of crisis.

Strategies for Managing Anxiety in a Tech-Driven World

Fortunately, there are many strategies for managing anxiety in a tech-driven world. Here are a few ideas:

1. Practice Mindfulness: Mindfulness is the practice of being present in the moment and non-judgmentally observing your thoughts and feelings. Mindfulness can be an effective way to manage anxiety because it helps you to become more aware of your thoughts and feelings, which can reduce their intensity. There are many apps and online resources available to help you learn mindfulness techniques, such as Headspace, Calm, and Insight Timer.

2. Set Boundaries: Setting boundaries around your use of technology can be an effective way to manage anxiety. For example, you might set limits on your social media use or designate certain times of day for checking email. You might also consider taking a break from technology altogether, such as by going on a technology-free retreat or spending time in nature.

3. Practice Self-Care: Self-care is essential for managing anxiety, regardless of the cause. Some self-care strategies that can be particularly effective for managing anxiety related to technology include getting enough sleep, eating a healthy diet, and engaging in physical activity. You might also consider other forms of self-care, such as meditation, yoga, or massage.

4. Seek Professional Help: If your anxiety is severe or interfering with your daily life, it's important to seek professional help. A mental health professional can help you develop an individualized treatment plan that may include therapy, medication, or a combination of both. They can also help you identify strategies for managing your anxiety in a tech-driven world.

The impact of digital devices and social media on anxiety levels

The rise of digital technology and social media has brought about significant changes in the way we communicate and interact with each other. While these advancements have undoubtedly brought numerous benefits, such as increased connectivity and accessibility, they have also been associated with certain negative effects, including an increase in anxiety levels. Below we will explore the impact of digital devices and social media on anxiety levels, as well as the ways in which individuals can mitigate these effects.

The relationship between technology and anxiety is complex and multifaceted. On the one hand, technology can be a source of comfort and support for those who struggle with anxiety. For example, there are numerous apps available that can help individuals manage their symptoms, such as meditation apps and breathing exercises. Additionally, online support groups and forums can provide a sense of community and belonging for those who may feel isolated or alone in their struggles.

On the other hand, technology can also be a significant source of stress and anxiety for many people. Social media, in particular, has been shown to have a significant impact on mental health. Research has found that frequent social media use can increase feelings of loneliness, anxiety, and depression. This is often due to the fact that social media presents an idealized version of life that is not reflective of reality, leading individuals to feel inadequate or insecure. Additionally, the constant pressure to present a perfect image online can lead to a fear of missing out (FOMO) and a sense of social comparison, both of which can contribute to anxiety levels.

In addition to social media, there are numerous other ways in which technology can contribute to anxiety levels. For example, the constant notifications and alerts from emails and messages can create a sense of urgency and make individuals feel as though they are always on call, even outside of work hours. Additionally, the 24/7 news cycle can create a constant sense of anxiety and stress, as individuals are bombarded with negative news stories and updates.

Given the potential negative effects of technology on anxiety levels, it is important for individuals to be mindful of their use and take steps to mitigate these effects. One way to do this is to set boundaries around technology use. This can involve setting specific times of day when technology is turned off, such as during meals or before bed. Additionally, individuals can set limits on their social media use, such as only checking their accounts at specific times of day or for a set amount of time.

Another way to mitigate the negative effects of technology on anxiety levels is to engage in activities that promote relaxation and stress reduction. This can involve engaging in mindfulness practices, such as meditation or yoga, or simply taking a break from technology and engaging in activities that promote relaxation, such as reading or taking a walk in nature.

Finally, it is important for individuals to seek out professional support if their anxiety levels are significantly impacting their daily functioning. This can involve seeking out therapy or counseling, which can help individuals develop coping strategies and learn how to manage their anxiety in a healthy way. Additionally, there are numerous resources available online and through mobile apps that can provide additional support and guidance.

Strategies for managing screen time and online interactions

In today's digital age, technology has become an integral part of our lives, and while it has brought numerous benefits, it has also brought some challenges. One of the most significant challenges is the impact of digital devices and social media on anxiety levels. With constant access to information, notifications, and messages, it's easy to become overwhelmed and stressed. However, there are ways to manage screen time and online interactions that can help reduce anxiety levels.

The first step in managing screen time and online interactions is to become aware of how much time you're spending on digital devices. This can be done by tracking your screen time using a smartphone app or a built-in feature on your device. Once you have an idea of how much time you're spending on your device, you can set goals to reduce your screen time gradually. For example, you might start by reducing your screen time by 30 minutes a day and gradually increase it over time.

Another strategy for managing screen time is to establish boundaries around technology use. For example, you might set a rule that you don't use your phone during meals or after a certain time at night. You could also establish technology-free zones in your home, such as the bedroom or the dinner table.

Social media can be a significant source of anxiety for many people, so it's essential to manage online interactions carefully. One way to do this is to limit your social media use. For example, you might choose to check your social media accounts once or twice a day instead of constantly scrolling through your feeds. You could also unfollow accounts that make you feel anxious or stressed and focus on following accounts that bring you joy and positivity.

It's also crucial to recognize that social media is not always an accurate representation of reality. People often present only the best parts of their lives on social media, which can make others feel inadequate or anxious. Remembering this can help put things into perspective and reduce anxiety levels.

Another way to manage online interactions is to practice digital detoxes. This means taking a break from social media and digital devices for a period of time, such as a weekend or a week. This can help reduce anxiety levels and provide a much-needed break from constant stimulation.

In addition to managing screen time and online interactions, there are other strategies that can help reduce anxiety levels related to technology. For example, practicing mindfulness and meditation can help increase self-awareness and reduce stress levels. Regular exercise, adequate sleep, and a healthy diet can also help improve overall mental health and reduce anxiety levels.

It's important to remember that technology is not inherently good or bad; it's how we use it that matters. By being mindful of our technology use and practicing healthy habits, we can reduce anxiety levels and enjoy the benefits of technology without the negative side effects.

Utilizing technology for anxiety relief and support

Utilizing Technology for Anxiety Relief and Support

In recent years, technology has become an increasingly popular tool for managing anxiety. With the rise of smartphones, wearable devices, and online platforms, people have more access than ever before to tools and resources for managing their mental health. From meditation apps to online support groups, there are countless ways that technology can be used to alleviate anxiety symptoms and provide support for those struggling with anxiety disorders. Below we will explore some of the ways in which technology can be utilized for anxiety relief and support.

One of the most popular and widely used tools for anxiety relief is meditation apps. These apps typically offer guided meditations, breathing exercises, and other mindfulness techniques that can help to calm the mind and reduce anxiety. Popular meditation apps include Headspace, Calm, and Insight Timer. These apps can be accessed on a smartphone or tablet, and many offer both free and paid versions.

Another way that technology can be utilized for anxiety relief is through virtual reality therapy. Virtual reality therapy involves using a headset to immerse oneself in a simulated environment. This technology is often used to treat anxiety disorders such as phobias and post-traumatic stress disorder (PTSD). For example, someone with a fear of flying might use virtual reality therapy to simulate a plane ride in a safe and controlled environment. This type of therapy can be incredibly effective, as it allows individuals to face their fears in a controlled and supportive environment.

Online support groups and forums are also an effective way to find support and understanding from others who are struggling with anxiety. These groups can be accessed from anywhere with an internet connection and provide a safe and supportive space for people to connect with others who understand what they are going through. Some popular online support groups for anxiety include the Anxiety and Depression Association of America (ADAA) support group, the Social Anxiety Support Group, and the Panic Disorder Support Group.

Technology can also be utilized for tracking and monitoring anxiety symptoms. There are many apps available that allow individuals to track their mood, anxiety levels, and other symptoms over time. This can be helpful in identifying triggers and patterns in anxiety symptoms, which can then be addressed through therapy or other interventions. Popular apps for tracking anxiety symptoms include Pacifica, MoodKit, and Stigma.

For those who prefer a more personalized approach, there are also online therapy platforms that offer virtual counseling sessions with licensed therapists. These platforms, such as BetterHelp and Talkspace, offer a convenient and accessible way for individuals to access therapy from the comfort of their own home. Online therapy can be particularly helpful for those who are unable to attend in-person sessions due to time constraints, mobility issues, or other factors.

While technology can be incredibly helpful for anxiety relief and support, it is important to recognize that it is not a substitute for professional treatment. If you are struggling with anxiety, it is important to seek help from a licensed mental health professional. Technology can be used in conjunction with therapy and other treatments to enhance their effectiveness, but it should not be used as a replacement for professional care.

Chapter Twenty-One

Coping with Health Anxiety

Coping with health anxiety can be a challenging and overwhelming experience for those who suffer from it. Health anxiety, also known as hypochondria or illness anxiety disorder, is characterized by excessive worry and fear about one's health, even when there is no apparent medical issue. This can lead to a range of physical and emotional symptoms, including panic attacks, avoidance of medical settings, and impairment in daily functioning. Below we will explore some coping strategies that can help individuals manage health anxiety and improve their quality of life.

The first step in coping with health anxiety is to educate oneself about the condition. Learning about the symptoms, causes, and treatment options can help reduce anxiety and increase feelings of control. It is important to recognize that health anxiety is a real condition that affects many people, and seeking help is not a sign of weakness. Seeking support from a mental health professional, such as a therapist or psychiatrist, can be beneficial in managing health anxiety. They can provide effective treatments such as cognitive-behavioral therapy (CBT) or medication to alleviate symptoms and develop healthy coping mechanisms.

Another coping strategy for health anxiety is to practice mindfulness and relaxation techniques. Mindfulness involves paying attention to the present moment without judgment, allowing one to focus on the here and now instead of worrying about the future. Relaxation techniques, such as deep breathing, progressive muscle relaxation, and yoga, can help reduce stress and promote a sense of calm. These techniques can be practiced anywhere, at any time, making them a useful tool for managing anxiety in everyday life.

Engaging in regular physical activity can also be beneficial for managing health anxiety. Exercise can help alleviate stress and anxiety by releasing endorphins, which are natural mood-boosters. Additionally, physical activity can promote a sense of accomplishment and control, which can be especially important for those with health anxiety. Finding an enjoyable physical activity, such as jogging, swimming, or yoga, can help make exercise a regular part of one's routine.

It is also important to practice good self-care when coping with health anxiety. This includes getting enough sleep, eating a healthy and balanced diet, and avoiding alcohol and drugs. Taking care of one's physical health can help reduce stress and anxiety, while also promoting overall well-being.

Another important coping strategy is to practice realistic thinking. Health anxiety often involves catastrophizing and overestimating the likelihood of medical issues. Practicing realistic thinking involves challenging these negative thoughts and replacing them with more balanced and realistic ones. For example, instead of assuming that a headache is a sign of a brain tumor, one could consider more likely explanations, such as stress or dehydration.

Finally, building a strong support network can be a crucial aspect of coping with health anxiety. This can involve reaching out to family and friends for emotional support, joining a support group for individuals with anxiety disorders, or seeking out online resources and forums. Having a support system can provide encouragement, validation, and understanding during difficult times.

Recognizing the signs of health anxiety

Health anxiety, also known as hypochondriasis or illness anxiety disorder, is a type of anxiety disorder that involves excessive and persistent worry about having a serious medical condition. Individuals with health anxiety may constantly check their body for symptoms, seek reassurance from others, and avoid situations or activities that they believe may trigger their anxiety.

Recognizing the signs of health anxiety is the first step in managing this condition. Some common symptoms of health anxiety include:

1. Preoccupation with physical symptoms: People with health anxiety tend to be excessively preoccupied with physical symptoms such as pain, discomfort, or abnormal sensations.

2. Constant checking and reassurance seeking: People with health anxiety may constantly check their body for signs of illness and seek reassurance from doctors, family, and friends.

3. Avoidance of medical appointments: Despite the preoccupation with physical symptoms, people with health anxiety may avoid medical appointments or tests out of fear that they will receive a serious diagnosis.

4. Excessive research: People with health anxiety may spend hours researching symptoms and medical conditions online, which can increase their anxiety and distress.

5. Interference with daily life: Health anxiety can interfere with daily life, leading to decreased social and occupational functioning.

If you or someone you know is experiencing these symptoms, it may be time to seek help from a mental health professional. A therapist can work with you to develop strategies for managing health anxiety and improving your overall well-being.

One important strategy for managing health anxiety is to develop a more balanced perspective on physical symptoms. This can involve learning to recognize and challenge anxious thoughts that may be fueling your worry. For example, if you notice yourself thinking "this headache must be a brain tumor," try to reframe this thought as "headaches are a common symptom and can be caused by many different things, including stress or lack of sleep."

Another helpful strategy is to practice relaxation techniques such as deep breathing, progressive muscle relaxation, or mindfulness meditation. These techniques can help to calm the body and reduce feelings of anxiety.

Cognitive-behavioral therapy (CBT) is a type of therapy that has been shown to be effective in treating health anxiety. CBT involves identifying and challenging negative thoughts and beliefs about health and illness, and learning coping skills to manage anxiety symptoms.

In some cases, medication may be recommended to help manage health anxiety. Antidepressant medications such as selective serotonin reuptake inhibitors (SSRIs) have been shown to be effective in reducing anxiety symptoms.

It is important to remember that health anxiety is a treatable condition. With the right support and strategies, individuals with health anxiety can learn to manage their symptoms and improve their overall quality of life. If you are struggling with health anxiety, consider reaching out to a mental health professional for support.

Strategies for managing health-related fears

Anxiety disorders are a common mental health issue, affecting millions of people around the world. One specific type of anxiety disorder is health anxiety, which is characterized by excessive worry about one's health and the fear of having a serious illness. This anxiety can lead to persistent and distressing symptoms that can negatively impact an individual's daily life, relationships, and overall well-being. Fortunately, there are strategies that can be implemented to help manage health-related fears and reduce the impact of health anxiety on one's life.

One effective strategy for managing health-related fears is cognitive-behavioral therapy (CBT). This type of therapy involves working with a mental health professional to identify and challenge negative thoughts and beliefs about one's health. The therapist will help the individual recognize the patterns of anxious thoughts and replace them with more rational and positive thoughts. This can help reduce anxiety and improve overall mental health.

Another useful strategy is to practice mindfulness meditation. Mindfulness involves paying attention to the present moment and accepting one's thoughts and feelings without judgment. Regular practice of mindfulness meditation can help individuals better manage their anxious thoughts and feelings, and reduce the impact of health anxiety on their daily life.

Exercise is also an effective way to manage health anxiety. Regular exercise has been shown to reduce anxiety and improve mood. It can also be a helpful distraction from anxious thoughts and feelings. Exercise can take many forms, such as going for a walk or run, practicing yoga, or taking a dance class. Finding an activity that is enjoyable and engaging can make it easier to incorporate exercise into one's daily routine.

In addition, it can be helpful to maintain a healthy lifestyle. Eating a balanced diet, getting enough sleep, and avoiding excessive alcohol or drug use can help reduce anxiety and improve overall health. Making small changes to one's daily routine, such as drinking more water or taking a few moments each day to relax, can also have a positive impact on one's mental health.

Another strategy is to seek support from others. Talking with a trusted friend or family member about one's health-related fears can provide a sense of relief and support. Joining a support group for individuals with anxiety or seeking professional counseling can also be beneficial. These resources can provide a safe and supportive environment for individuals to share their experiences and learn coping strategies from others.

Finally, it is important to remember that seeking medical care is essential for managing health anxiety. Regular check-ups with a healthcare provider can provide reassurance and help identify any potential health concerns. However, it is important to avoid excessive or unnecessary medical testing, as this can further fuel health anxiety.

Navigating the healthcare system

1. Navigating the Healthcare System: Strategies for Managing Anxiety

When it comes to managing anxiety, seeking support and treatment from healthcare professionals is often essential. However, for many individuals, navigating the healthcare system can be a daunting and overwhelming experience in itself. From finding a provider to accessing affordable care, there are many barriers that can make it difficult to receive the care and support needed to manage anxiety. Below we will explore some strategies for navigating the healthcare system and managing anxiety effectively.

Finding the Right Provider

One of the first steps in managing anxiety is finding the right healthcare provider. This can be a challenging task, as not all providers have experience or training in treating anxiety disorders. To start, it may be helpful to research providers who specialize in anxiety disorders or have experience treating patients with similar symptoms. Reading online reviews and asking for referrals from friends, family, or other healthcare providers can also be helpful.

Another factor to consider when seeking a healthcare provider is insurance coverage. Understanding the terms of your insurance policy and the costs associated with different providers can help you make an informed decision and avoid unexpected medical bills. Some providers may also offer sliding scale fees or payment plans for those who are uninsured or underinsured.

Preparing for Appointments

Once you have found a healthcare provider, it is important to prepare for appointments in order to make the most of your time with them. This can include making a list of symptoms, concerns, and questions to bring to the appointment. Being honest and open about your experiences with anxiety can help your provider create an individualized treatment plan that meets your unique needs.

It can also be helpful to bring a trusted friend or family member to appointments for support and to help you remember important information. Some healthcare providers may also offer telemedicine appointments, which can be a convenient option for those who have difficulty leaving home or traveling to appointments.

Accessing Affordable Care

For many individuals, accessing affordable healthcare can be a significant barrier to managing anxiety. It is important to understand the options available for accessing care and to advocate for yourself to ensure you receive the care you need.

If you have insurance, it can be helpful to research your benefits and understand your copays, deductibles, and out-of-pocket costs. Some insurance plans may offer coverage for mental health services, while others may require prior authorization or impose limits on the number of sessions covered.

For those who are uninsured or underinsured, there are still options for accessing affordable care. Many healthcare providers offer sliding scale fees or payment plans for those who are unable to pay the full cost of treatment. Non-profit organizations and community health centers may also offer low-cost or free mental health services.

Self-Care and Support

While healthcare providers can offer valuable support and treatment for anxiety, it is also important to practice self-care and seek support from loved ones. This can include engaging in activities that promote relaxation and stress relief, such as yoga, meditation, or deep breathing exercises. Building a strong support system of friends, family, or support groups can also provide a sense of connection and understanding during difficult times.

In addition, it can be helpful to stay informed about new research and treatment options for anxiety. Educating yourself about anxiety disorders and treatment options can help you make informed decisions about your care and feel empowered in your recovery journey.

Chapter Twenty-Two

Resilience and Personal Growth

Resilience and personal growth are concepts that are closely tied to anxiety disorders. While anxiety can be a debilitating condition, it can also provide opportunities for growth and development. Resilience is the ability to bounce back from adversity, while personal growth is the process of learning and adapting to challenges. Below we will explore the relationship between anxiety, resilience, and personal growth.

Anxiety disorders are among the most common mental health conditions, affecting millions of people worldwide. These disorders can manifest in a variety of ways, including panic attacks, social anxiety, generalized anxiety disorder, obsessive-compulsive disorder, and post-traumatic stress disorder. Anxiety can be caused by a wide range of factors, including genetics, environment, life events, and brain chemistry.

While anxiety can be a challenging condition to live with, it can also be an opportunity for growth. Individuals with anxiety often develop resilience as a result of their experiences. Resilience is the ability to adapt to and recover from stressful situations. It is not a fixed trait, but rather a skill that can be developed over time. People with anxiety disorders may become more resilient as they learn to cope with their symptoms.

Resilience is not simply about bouncing back from adversity. It also involves the ability to learn from challenging experiences and to use that knowledge to develop new skills and strengths. People with anxiety disorders may learn new coping strategies, develop better communication skills, or become more self-aware as a result of their experiences. These skills can be valuable in all areas of life, not just in managing anxiety.

Personal growth is another potential outcome of living with anxiety. Personal growth involves learning, developing new skills, and making positive changes in one's life. People with anxiety may become more introspective and self-aware as they work to manage their symptoms. They may also develop new interests or hobbies, or find ways to connect with others who share their experiences.

One of the keys to personal growth is self-compassion. People with anxiety often struggle with feelings of shame, guilt, or self-criticism. Developing self-compassion involves being kind and understanding toward oneself, even when experiencing difficult emotions or challenging situations. It can be a powerful tool for managing anxiety and promoting personal growth.

There are many strategies that can help individuals with anxiety to develop resilience and promote personal growth. Some of these include:

1. Mindfulness: Mindfulness involves being present in the moment and non-judgmentally observing one's thoughts and feelings. It can be a useful tool for managing anxiety symptoms and promoting resilience.

2. Cognitive-behavioral therapy: Cognitive-behavioral therapy (CBT) is a type of therapy that focuses on changing negative thought patterns and behaviors. It can be a highly effective treatment for anxiety disorders.

3. Social support: Having a supportive network of friends and family can be an important factor in promoting resilience and personal growth.

4. Self-care: Taking care of oneself physically, emotionally, and mentally can help to manage anxiety symptoms and promote personal growth.

5. Education: Learning about anxiety disorders and their treatment can help individuals to better understand and manage their symptoms.

Cultivating a growth mindset

Cultivating a growth mindset is a powerful tool in overcoming anxiety disorders. A growth mindset is the belief that one's abilities and intelligence can be developed and improved over time through effort, practice, and perseverance. It is the opposite of a fixed mindset, which assumes that one's abilities and intelligence are fixed and unchangeable. Those with a growth mindset are more likely to embrace challenges, learn from failures, and persist in the face of setbacks.

Individuals with anxiety disorders often struggle with negative self-talk and limiting beliefs, which can contribute to feelings of helplessness and hopelessness. Cultivating a growth mindset can help individuals challenge these negative thought patterns and develop a more positive and resilient mindset. By embracing challenges and viewing setbacks as opportunities for growth, individuals can develop greater self-confidence and self-esteem.

One effective way to cultivate a growth mindset is through the practice of mindfulness. Mindfulness is the practice of being fully present in the moment and observing one's thoughts and feelings without judgment. By practicing mindfulness, individuals can become more aware of their thought patterns and begin to challenge negative self-talk. This can help individuals develop a more positive and realistic self-image, which can in turn lead to greater self-confidence and self-esteem.

Another way to cultivate a growth mindset is through goal-setting. Setting realistic and achievable goals can help individuals develop a sense of purpose and direction, as well as provide motivation to persist in the face of challenges. It is important to set goals that are specific, measurable, and achievable, as well as to break larger goals down into smaller, more manageable steps.

In addition to mindfulness and goal-setting, it is important for individuals to develop a support system of family, friends, and professionals who can provide encouragement and guidance. Support groups and therapy can also be helpful in providing a safe and supportive environment for individuals to share their experiences and receive feedback and support.

Embracing vulnerability

Anxiety disorders are characterized by excessive and persistent worry, fear, or anxiety that interferes with daily life. One of the challenges of living with an anxiety disorder is feeling like you have to put on a brave face all the time and not show any vulnerability. However, embracing vulnerability can actually be a key to managing anxiety and building resilience.

Vulnerability is often associated with weakness or the potential for harm, but in reality, vulnerability is a natural and necessary part of being human. It means acknowledging and expressing our true feelings, needs, and fears, and being open to the possibility of being hurt or rejected. While vulnerability can be uncomfortable or scary, it also has the potential to connect us with others, foster empathy and understanding, and help us grow and learn from our experiences.

For people with anxiety disorders, the fear of being vulnerable can be especially strong. Anxiety often leads to a desire for control and predictability, which can make it difficult to let down one's guard and reveal true thoughts and feelings. However, the act of opening up and sharing vulnerabilities can actually be liberating and empowering.

One way to embrace vulnerability is through self-compassion. This means treating oneself with kindness and understanding, as one would treat a close friend who is going through a difficult time. It involves acknowledging that everyone has flaws and makes mistakes, and accepting oneself as imperfect but worthy of love and respect.

Another way to embrace vulnerability is by sharing one's struggles with trusted friends or family members. Talking about one's fears and anxieties can help to normalize them, and can also lead to practical advice or support. It can also help to reduce feelings of shame or isolation that often accompany anxiety.

Group therapy can be a particularly effective way to embrace vulnerability in a supportive and understanding environment. In group therapy, individuals with similar struggles come together to share their experiences and support one another. The group provides a safe space for individuals to practice vulnerability and learn from one another.

Finally, embracing vulnerability can also mean being open to new experiences and taking risks. While this can be scary for people with anxiety, it can also lead to personal growth and increased resilience. Taking small steps outside of one's comfort zone, such as trying a new hobby or talking to a stranger, can help to build confidence and reduce fear.

Mindfulness and Anxiety

Anxiety disorders affect millions of people worldwide, and the impact can be debilitating. Living with anxiety can be a challenging experience, but there are ways to manage it effectively. One approach that has gained popularity in recent years is mindfulness.

Mindfulness is a practice that involves paying attention to the present moment in a non-judgmental way. It is a way of focusing the mind and becoming more aware of one's thoughts, feelings, and surroundings. Mindfulness-based interventions have been shown to be effective in reducing symptoms of anxiety and improving overall well-being.

Anxiety is often characterized by racing thoughts, worries about the future, and physical sensations such as tension or restlessness. Mindfulness can help individuals with anxiety to become more aware of their thoughts and physical sensations and to develop a more accepting and non-judgmental attitude towards them.

Research has shown that mindfulness can be helpful in treating a range of anxiety disorders, including generalized anxiety disorder, social anxiety disorder, and panic disorder. In one study, participants with generalized anxiety disorder who completed a mindfulness-based stress reduction program showed significant reductions in anxiety symptoms and improvements in overall functioning.

Mindfulness can also be helpful for individuals with social anxiety disorder, which is characterized by intense fear of social situations. In one study, participants who completed a mindfulness-based intervention showed significant improvements in social anxiety symptoms and were more likely to engage in social activities.

For individuals with panic disorder, mindfulness can be helpful in reducing the frequency and intensity of panic attacks. In one study, participants who completed a mindfulness-based intervention showed significant reductions in panic symptoms and improvements in overall well-being.

There are several ways to practice mindfulness, including mindfulness meditation, body scan, and mindful breathing. Mindfulness meditation involves focusing the attention on a specific object, such as the breath, and bringing the mind back to that object whenever the mind wanders. Body scan involves focusing on each part of the body in turn and noticing any physical sensations without judgment. Mindful breathing involves paying attention to the breath and noticing how it feels as it enters and leaves the body.

In addition to formal mindfulness practices, individuals can incorporate mindfulness into their daily lives by paying attention to the present moment during routine activities such as eating, showering, or walking. This can help to cultivate a more mindful and present-focused mindset, which can be helpful in managing anxiety symptoms.

The benefits of mindfulness practices for individuals with anxiety disorders

The fast-paced and constantly changing world can cause a significant amount of stress and anxiety for many individuals. In fact, anxiety disorders are the most common mental health disorders in the United States, affecting nearly 40 million adults annually. Fortunately, there are various ways to manage anxiety, and one approach that has gained popularity in recent years is mindfulness.

Mindfulness is a form of meditation that involves being fully present and aware of your thoughts, feelings, and surroundings in a nonjudgmental way. It is often used as a tool for stress reduction and relaxation, but it can also be an effective strategy for managing anxiety disorders.

One of the primary benefits of mindfulness for individuals with anxiety disorders is its ability to promote relaxation and decrease physiological symptoms of anxiety, such as rapid heart rate, muscle tension, and sweating. By focusing on the present moment and letting go of worry about the future or regrets about the past, mindfulness can help calm the body's stress response and reduce the intensity of anxiety symptoms.

Additionally, mindfulness can help individuals with anxiety disorders learn to identify and accept their anxious thoughts and feelings without getting caught up in them. This is known as "mindful acceptance," and it involves acknowledging and experiencing difficult emotions without trying to suppress or avoid them. By practicing mindful acceptance, individuals can learn to observe their anxious thoughts and feelings without getting overwhelmed by them or feeling the need to react impulsively.

Mindfulness can also improve overall emotional regulation and enhance coping skills. By learning to stay present and nonjudgmental, individuals can develop greater emotional awareness and better recognize when they are feeling stressed or overwhelmed. This heightened awareness can then help them make more deliberate and effective decisions when faced with difficult situations.

In addition to these benefits, mindfulness has been shown to be effective in treating various anxiety disorders. For example, mindfulness-based stress reduction (MBSR) is a program that has been shown to be effective in reducing symptoms of generalized anxiety disorder, panic disorder, and social anxiety disorder. MBSR typically involves weekly classes and daily at-home practice, and it focuses on developing mindfulness skills through meditation, body awareness, and gentle yoga.

Another mindfulness-based program that has shown promise in treating anxiety disorders is mindfulness-based cognitive therapy (MBCT). MBCT is designed specifically for individuals with recurrent depression, but it has also been shown to be effective in reducing symptoms of generalized anxiety disorder, social anxiety disorder, and panic disorder. MBCT involves both mindfulness practice and cognitive therapy techniques, such as identifying and challenging negative thought patterns.

In addition to formal mindfulness programs, there are many simple mindfulness techniques that individuals with anxiety disorders can use in their daily lives. For example, taking a few minutes to focus on deep breathing, paying attention to the physical sensations of the breath as it enters and leaves the body, can help calm the mind and reduce stress.

Another technique is to practice mindful observation, simply noticing and describing the sights, sounds, smells, and other sensations in the present moment without judgment or analysis. This can be a helpful way to shift attention away from anxious thoughts and feelings and toward the present moment.

Incorporating mindfulness into daily routines

Anxiety disorders are a common mental health condition affecting many people around the world. While there are various treatments available, incorporating mindfulness practices into daily routines has gained popularity as an effective tool for managing anxiety symptoms. Below we will explore the benefits of mindfulness practices and how they can be incorporated into daily routines to help individuals with anxiety disorders.

Mindfulness refers to the practice of paying attention to the present moment without judgment. It is an ancient practice derived from Buddhist meditation and has been shown to have numerous benefits for mental health. One of the main benefits of mindfulness practices is that they can help individuals manage anxiety symptoms. When we are anxious, we tend to worry about the future or ruminate on past events. Mindfulness practices can help individuals break this cycle by bringing their attention to the present moment.

Research has shown that mindfulness practices can reduce symptoms of anxiety by reducing activity in the amygdala, the part of the brain responsible for processing fear and anxiety. By reducing amygdala activity, individuals may experience less anxiety and feel more in control of their thoughts and emotions.

Incorporating mindfulness practices into daily routines can be a simple and effective way to manage anxiety symptoms. One way to do this is by practicing mindfulness meditation. This involves finding a quiet place to sit, focusing on your breath, and bringing your attention back to your breath whenever your mind wanders. By doing this regularly, individuals may develop greater awareness of their thoughts and emotions, and learn to observe them without judgment.

Another way to incorporate mindfulness into daily routines is through mindfulness-based stress reduction (MBSR) techniques. MBSR is a structured program that teaches individuals how to incorporate mindfulness practices into their daily lives. This program typically involves attending weekly group sessions and practicing various mindfulness techniques, such as body scans, yoga, and walking meditation.

In addition to formal mindfulness practices, individuals can also incorporate mindfulness into daily activities. For example, when taking a shower, individuals can focus on the sensation of the water on their skin and the smell of the soap. When eating a meal, individuals can focus on the taste and texture of the food. By doing this, individuals can bring their attention to the present moment and reduce anxiety-provoking thoughts and worries.

Incorporating mindfulness into daily routines can also help individuals develop resilience and coping skills. When we are anxious, we tend to focus on negative thoughts and emotions. By practicing mindfulness, individuals can learn to observe these thoughts and emotions without judgment and develop a greater sense of self-awareness. This can help individuals build resilience and develop coping skills to manage anxiety symptoms.

Furthermore, mindfulness practices can also improve overall well-being. Research has shown that mindfulness practices can improve sleep, reduce symptoms of depression, and improve overall quality of life. By incorporating mindfulness into daily routines, individuals may experience not only a reduction in anxiety symptoms but also an overall improvement in their mental health and well-being.

Mindfulness techniques specifically designed for anxiety

Mindfulness is a practice that involves paying attention to the present moment without judgment. It has been shown to be effective in reducing symptoms of anxiety and improving overall mental health. For those with anxiety disorders, mindfulness can be particularly helpful in managing symptoms and increasing resilience. Below we will explore some mindfulness techniques specifically designed for anxiety.

One mindfulness technique that is particularly helpful for anxiety is called "grounding." Grounding involves focusing on your physical senses to help you feel more present and grounded in the moment. To practice grounding, take a few deep breaths and then start to focus on your senses. Notice what you can see, hear, feel, smell, and taste. You might focus on the feeling of your feet on the ground, the sounds of birds chirping, the smell of fresh air, or the taste of a mint. Grounding can be done anywhere, at any time, and is a quick and effective way to bring yourself back to the present moment.

Another mindfulness technique that is helpful for anxiety is called "body scanning." Body scanning involves bringing your attention to different parts of your body and noticing any sensations you feel. To practice body scanning, find a comfortable position and close your eyes. Take a few deep breaths and then start to bring your attention to the top of your head. Notice any sensations you feel in this area, such as tingling or tightness. Then, move your attention down to your face and neck, shoulders, arms, hands, chest, back, abdomen, hips, legs, and feet, noticing any sensations in each area. Body scanning can help you become more aware of how your body feels and can help you identify areas of tension or discomfort that you may not have been aware of.

1. Another mindfulness technique that can be helpful for anxiety is called "loving-kindness meditation." Loving-kindness meditation involves focusing on feelings of love, kindness, and compassion toward yourself and others. To practice loving-kindness meditation, find a quiet and comfortable place to sit. Close your eyes and take a few deep breaths. Then, repeat the following phrases to yourself, silently or out loud: "May I be happy. May I be healthy. May I be safe. May I live with ease." After repeating these phrases to yourself for a few minutes, start to extend these feelings of love and kindness to others. You might choose someone you care about, someone who has been kind to you, or someone you are having difficulty with. Repeat the same phrases to this person: "May you be happy. May you be healthy. May you be safe. May you live with ease." Loving-kindness meditation can help you cultivate feelings of warmth and kindness, which can counteract feelings of anxiety and fear.

Finally, another mindfulness technique that is helpful for anxiety is called "breath awareness." Breath awareness involves focusing on your breath and observing it without judgment. To practice breath awareness, find a comfortable position and close your eyes. Take a few deep breaths and then start to focus on your breath. Notice the sensation of the breath as it enters and exits your body. You might focus on the feeling of the air moving in and out of your nose, the rise and fall of your chest, or the sensation of your diaphragm moving up and down. If your mind starts to wander, gently bring your attention back to your breath. Breath awareness can help you calm your mind and reduce feelings of anxiety.

Chapter Twenty-Three

Sleep and Anxiety

Sleep and Anxiety

Anxiety is a common mental health issue that affects millions of people worldwide. It can manifest in various forms, including generalized anxiety disorder, social anxiety disorder, panic disorder, and others. Anxiety can cause several physical and emotional symptoms, such as restlessness, irritability, fear, and difficulty concentrating. One area that anxiety can significantly impact is sleep. Below we will explore the relationship between sleep and anxiety and the importance of sleep in managing anxiety.

Anxiety and Sleep

Sleep and anxiety have a complicated relationship. On the one hand, anxiety can cause insomnia or difficulty falling asleep, staying asleep, or waking up too early. This phenomenon is commonly known as anxiety-induced insomnia. On the other hand, a lack of sleep can exacerbate anxiety symptoms, leading to a vicious cycle of anxiety and sleep deprivation.

Anxiety can affect sleep in several ways. For instance, anxious thoughts can cause racing thoughts, making it challenging to fall asleep. Additionally, anxiety can cause physical symptoms such as increased heart rate and rapid breathing, making it difficult to relax and fall asleep. In some cases, anxiety can also cause nightmares or night terrors, leading to disrupted sleep.

Sleep, Anxiety, and Physical Health

The impact of sleep on mental health, particularly anxiety, cannot be overstated. Research has shown that people who suffer from anxiety disorders often experience poor sleep quality and quantity. This lack of sleep can have severe consequences on both physical and mental health. Sleep is critical for the body to function correctly, and sleep deprivation can lead to various physical health issues such as obesity, diabetes, high blood pressure, and cardiovascular disease.

Sleep deprivation can also affect mental health. People who experience sleep disturbances are more likely to develop anxiety disorders or depression. It can also make it challenging to manage existing anxiety symptoms. Therefore, treating sleep problems is essential in managing anxiety and improving overall mental and physical health.

Managing Anxiety through Sleep

To manage anxiety, it is essential to establish healthy sleep habits. Here are some strategies for improving sleep quality and quantity:

1. Establish a regular sleep schedule: Going to bed and waking up at the same time every day can help regulate your body's internal clock, making it easier to fall asleep and wake up.

2. Create a relaxing bedtime routine: Engage in relaxing activities before bedtime, such as taking a warm bath, reading, or listening to calming music.

3. Avoid stimulants: Caffeine, alcohol, and nicotine can all interfere with sleep, so it is best to avoid these substances before bedtime.

4. Create a comfortable sleep environment: Make sure your bedroom is cool, dark, and quiet to promote restful sleep.

5. Practice mindfulness: Engage in mindfulness practices such as meditation or deep breathing exercises to help calm the mind and relax the body before bedtime.

6. Seek professional help: If sleep problems persist, it is essential to seek professional help from a qualified healthcare provider.

The impact of anxiety on sleep patterns and quality

Anxiety disorders are a common mental health condition affecting millions of people worldwide. While anxiety can affect individuals in different ways, one of the most common symptoms is sleep disturbance. Below we will explore the impact of anxiety on sleep patterns and quality, as well as strategies for improving sleep in individuals with anxiety disorders.

1. Anxiety and Sleep: The Connection

Anxiety can have a significant impact on sleep, both in terms of sleep quality and quantity. Anxiety can cause racing thoughts, physical sensations such as restlessness and muscle tension, and an overall sense of agitation or unease. These symptoms can make it challenging for individuals with anxiety to fall asleep, stay asleep, and achieve restorative sleep.

One of the most common sleep disorders associated with anxiety is insomnia. Insomnia is characterized by difficulty falling asleep or staying asleep, waking up too early, or feeling unrefreshed upon waking. Insomnia can be a vicious cycle; anxiety can lead to difficulty falling asleep, and poor sleep quality can exacerbate anxiety symptoms.

Anxiety can also impact the circadian rhythm, the body's natural sleep-wake cycle. Individuals with anxiety may experience delayed or disrupted sleep-wake patterns, leading to fatigue during the day and difficulty falling asleep at night. This disruption can further contribute to sleep disturbance and worsen anxiety symptoms.

Strategies for Improving Sleep in Individuals with Anxiety Disorders

Fortunately, there are several strategies individuals with anxiety disorders can use to improve their sleep quality and quantity. These strategies include:

2. Relaxation techniques: Relaxation techniques, such as deep breathing exercises, progressive muscle relaxation, and visualization, can help calm the mind and body, reduce physical tension, and promote relaxation.

3. Cognitive-behavioral therapy: Cognitive-behavioral therapy (CBT) is a form of therapy that can help individuals with anxiety identify and change negative thought patterns and behaviors that contribute to anxiety symptoms, including sleep disturbance.

4. Sleep hygiene: Establishing healthy sleep habits, such as maintaining a consistent sleep schedule, avoiding caffeine and alcohol before bedtime, and creating a relaxing sleep environment, can improve sleep quality and quantity.

5. Medication: Certain medications, such as benzodiazepines and antidepressants, can help alleviate anxiety symptoms and improve sleep quality. However, it's important to work with a healthcare provider to determine the most appropriate medication and dosage.

6. Mindfulness practices: Mindfulness practices, such as meditation and yoga, can help individuals with anxiety develop greater self-awareness, reduce stress and anxiety symptoms, and improve sleep quality.

Strategies for improving sleep hygiene and addressing sleep disorders

Strategies for improving sleep hygiene and addressing sleep disorders can be an essential part of managing anxiety disorders. Anxiety can cause disrupted sleep patterns, which can further exacerbate feelings of stress and anxiety. Below we will explore some of the strategies that can be used to improve sleep hygiene and address sleep disorders in individuals with anxiety disorders.

One of the first steps in improving sleep hygiene is to establish a consistent sleep schedule. Going to bed and waking up at the same time every day can help regulate the body's internal clock and improve overall sleep quality. It is recommended that adults aim for 7-9 hours of sleep each night. Establishing a bedtime routine that includes relaxation techniques such as meditation, deep breathing exercises, or gentle stretching can also be beneficial.

Creating a sleep-conducive environment can also be helpful. The bedroom should be quiet, cool, and dark. It is also recommended to keep electronic devices out of the bedroom as the blue light they emit can interfere with the body's production of melatonin, a hormone that promotes sleep.

Reducing caffeine and alcohol intake can also have a positive impact on sleep quality. Caffeine is a stimulant that can disrupt sleep, so it is recommended to avoid consuming it in the afternoon or evening. Alcohol may make an individual feel drowsy initially, but it can disrupt sleep later in the night, leading to poorer quality sleep.

Another factor that can impact sleep hygiene is exercise. Regular exercise can improve overall health and reduce feelings of anxiety, which can, in turn, improve sleep quality. However, it is recommended to avoid vigorous exercise close to bedtime as it can increase the body's alertness, making it more difficult to fall asleep.

Addressing sleep disorders such as insomnia or sleep apnea can also be important in managing anxiety disorders. Insomnia is characterized by difficulty falling or staying asleep, while sleep apnea is a condition where an individual's breathing repeatedly stops and starts during sleep. Both of these conditions can lead to disrupted sleep, which can exacerbate anxiety symptoms.

Cognitive-behavioral therapy (CBT) is an evidence-based approach that has been shown to be effective in addressing sleep disorders. CBT for insomnia focuses on identifying and changing negative thought patterns and behaviors that contribute to sleep problems. It may also involve techniques such as sleep restriction therapy, where an individual's time in bed is limited to improve sleep efficiency.

In some cases, medication may also be prescribed to manage sleep disorders. Sleep aids such as benzodiazepines or non-benzodiazepine hypnotics can be effective in the short term but can lead to dependence and should be used with caution.

The role of sleep in overall anxiety management

Anxiety disorders are prevalent and can have a significant impact on an individual's quality of life. One aspect that can exacerbate anxiety symptoms is poor sleep. Sleep and anxiety have a complex and reciprocal relationship, as anxiety can interfere with sleep and poor sleep can exacerbate anxiety symptoms. Therefore, understanding the role of sleep in anxiety management is crucial in treating anxiety disorders.

The Impact of Anxiety on Sleep Patterns and Quality

Anxiety can affect the quality and quantity of sleep. Individuals with anxiety disorders often report difficulty falling asleep, staying asleep, and waking up too early. They may also experience nightmares, night sweats, and other sleep disturbances. Anxiety can cause racing thoughts and a hyperactive mind, which makes it difficult to relax and fall asleep. Additionally, individuals with anxiety disorders may worry about their sleep quality, further exacerbating sleep disturbances.

The reciprocal relationship between anxiety and sleep is also important to note. Poor sleep can worsen anxiety symptoms, which can then lead to further sleep disturbances. Lack of sleep can also make it more challenging to cope with stressful situations, leading to increased anxiety levels.

Strategies for Improving Sleep Hygiene and Addressing Sleep Disorders

Improving sleep hygiene can be an effective way to manage anxiety symptoms. Sleep hygiene refers to the habits and practices that promote healthy sleep patterns. These can include:

1. Establishing a regular sleep schedule: Going to bed and waking up at the same time every day can help regulate the body's internal clock, making it easier to fall asleep and stay asleep.

2. Creating a sleep-conducive environment: The bedroom should be cool, dark, and quiet. Avoid using electronics before bed, as the blue light emitted by screens can interfere with sleep.

3. Practicing relaxation techniques: Relaxation techniques such as deep breathing, progressive muscle relaxation, and meditation can help reduce anxiety levels and promote relaxation before bedtime.

4. Engaging in regular exercise: Exercise can promote better sleep quality and reduce anxiety symptoms.

5. Avoiding caffeine and alcohol: Caffeine and alcohol can interfere with sleep quality, making it more difficult to fall asleep and stay asleep.

For individuals with sleep disorders, seeking treatment may be necessary. Treatments can include therapy, medication, and other interventions to address underlying sleep disorders such as insomnia or sleep apnea.

The Role of Sleep in Overall Anxiety Management

Addressing sleep disturbances can be an essential component of anxiety management. Poor sleep quality can exacerbate anxiety symptoms, making it more challenging to manage anxiety effectively. By improving sleep hygiene and addressing sleep disorders, individuals with anxiety disorders can improve their overall quality of life and reduce anxiety symptoms.

Additionally, regular, quality sleep can promote emotional regulation, which can be helpful in managing anxiety symptoms. When an individual is well-rested, they are better equipped to manage stressors and handle challenging situations.

Incorporating healthy sleep habits into an overall treatment plan for anxiety can be effective in reducing anxiety symptoms and improving overall mental health. It is crucial to consult with a healthcare professional to develop a personalized treatment plan that addresses both anxiety and sleep disturbances.

Chapter Twenty-Four

Nutrition and Exercise

Anxiety disorders affect millions of people around the world, and managing this condition can be challenging. In addition to therapy and medication, lifestyle changes like diet and exercise can also be useful in managing anxiety. While these factors are often overlooked in the treatment of anxiety, they can play a significant role in improving mental health.

Diet is one of the critical factors that affect our overall health, and the same holds for mental health. Nutritional deficiencies can cause mood disturbances and anxiety symptoms. In contrast, a healthy and balanced diet can have a calming effect on the mind and help manage anxiety symptoms. A diet high in sugar, caffeine, and processed foods can lead to mood swings and anxiety. These foods can interfere with the body's ability to regulate blood sugar, leading to energy crashes and increased anxiety.

On the other hand, a diet rich in whole foods, fruits, and vegetables can help regulate blood sugar and promote a calm mind. Some specific nutrients have been shown to have a beneficial effect on anxiety, such as omega-3 fatty acids, magnesium, and vitamin B complex. Omega-3 fatty acids are found in fatty fish, flaxseeds, and chia seeds and can help reduce inflammation in the brain, which is linked to anxiety. Magnesium is essential for relaxation and can be found in dark leafy greens, nuts, and seeds. Vitamin B complex, which includes thiamine, riboflavin, and niacin, helps regulate the nervous system and can be found in whole grains, legumes, and leafy greens.

Exercise is also an essential aspect of managing anxiety. Exercise releases endorphins, which are natural chemicals that improve mood and promote relaxation. It also helps reduce muscle tension, which can be a physical manifestation of anxiety. Exercise can take many forms, from yoga and pilates to running and weightlifting. The key is to find an exercise routine that works for you and can be sustained long-term.

Regular exercise has been shown to reduce anxiety symptoms, improve mood, and increase self-esteem. It also promotes better sleep, which can be particularly beneficial for those with anxiety. Exercise doesn't have to be strenuous; even light exercise like walking or stretching can have a positive impact on mental health.

In addition to diet and exercise, other lifestyle changes can help manage anxiety. Stress reduction techniques such as meditation, deep breathing exercises, and mindfulness can be effective in reducing anxiety symptoms. These practices help train the mind to focus on the present moment and can reduce anxious thoughts and feelings.

Adequate sleep is also essential in managing anxiety. Lack of sleep can cause irritability, mood swings, and fatigue, all of which can exacerbate anxiety symptoms. Getting enough sleep, ideally seven to eight hours per night, can improve mood, reduce stress, and promote overall well-being.

The role of diet and nutrition in managing anxiety symptoms

Anxiety disorders affect millions of people worldwide, and their symptoms can be debilitating, affecting every aspect of life. While therapy and medication are essential components of treatment, lifestyle modifications can also play a crucial role in managing anxiety symptoms. Two important lifestyle factors that can help alleviate anxiety symptoms are diet and nutrition.

Diet and nutrition are often overlooked as part of an overall anxiety management plan. Still, several studies have shown a clear link between food choices and anxiety levels. One study published in the Journal of Psychiatric Research found that a diet high in processed foods and sugar was associated with a higher prevalence of anxiety and depression. In contrast, a diet rich in whole foods, such as fruits, vegetables, and whole grains, was associated with a lower risk of anxiety and depression.

Several nutrients have also been linked to anxiety management. For example, the B vitamins, including B12, folate, and B6, play a crucial role in brain function and may help reduce anxiety symptoms. Omega-3 fatty acids, found in fish, nuts, and seeds, have also been found to have a calming effect on the brain.

Additionally, some studies have shown that certain herbal supplements can help manage anxiety symptoms. For example, the herb passionflower has been found to have a calming effect on the brain and may help reduce anxiety levels. Similarly, the herb kava has been found to have anxiolytic effects and may help reduce anxiety symptoms.

Along with diet and nutrition, exercise is another important lifestyle factor that can help manage anxiety symptoms. Exercise has been shown to have a powerful impact on anxiety levels, with regular physical activity associated with reduced anxiety levels. Exercise helps reduce stress hormones, such as cortisol, while increasing the production of feel-good hormones, such as endorphins. Additionally, regular exercise can help improve sleep, another critical factor in anxiety management.

The type of exercise that is most effective for anxiety management varies from person to person. Some people may prefer high-intensity workouts, such as running or cycling, while others may find more gentle exercise, such as yoga or Pilates, more effective. Ultimately, finding an exercise routine that feels enjoyable and sustainable is key.

While diet and exercise can be powerful tools in anxiety management, it is essential to remember that they are just one piece of the puzzle. It is crucial to work with a mental health professional to develop a comprehensive anxiety management plan that addresses all aspects of the condition.

The benefits of physical activity for mental health

Anxiety disorders are a common mental health issue affecting millions of people worldwide. While medication and therapy are commonly used to treat these disorders, recent research suggests that physical activity can also be beneficial in managing anxiety symptoms. Below we will explore the benefits of exercise for mental health and its role in managing anxiety.

There is growing evidence to suggest that regular physical activity can have a positive impact on mental health. Exercise has been shown to reduce symptoms of depression and anxiety, as well as improve overall mood and quality of life. The mechanisms behind these benefits are not yet fully understood, but research suggests that exercise may increase the production of endorphins, the body's natural mood-enhancing chemicals. Exercise can also reduce inflammation, improve sleep, and increase self-esteem, all of which can contribute to a reduction in anxiety symptoms.

When it comes to anxiety disorders specifically, exercise has been found to be particularly effective in managing symptoms. Studies have shown that regular physical activity can reduce the severity of anxiety symptoms, such as worry and tension, in people with generalized anxiety disorder (GAD). Exercise has also been found to be beneficial for people with panic disorder and social anxiety disorder.

One of the ways in which exercise can help manage anxiety is through its ability to provide a distraction from anxious thoughts. When we exercise, we focus our attention on our bodies and the physical sensations we are experiencing, rather than our worries and fears. This can help break the cycle of anxious thoughts and feelings, and provide a temporary relief from anxiety symptoms.

Another way in which exercise can help manage anxiety is through its ability to reduce stress. Stress is a common trigger for anxiety symptoms, and exercise has been shown to be effective in reducing stress levels. Exercise can also help regulate the body's stress response system, making us more resilient to stressful situations.

In addition to its immediate benefits, regular exercise can also lead to long-term improvements in mental health. Studies have shown that people who engage in regular physical activity are less likely to develop anxiety and depression later in life. Exercise can also improve self-esteem and confidence, making us more resilient to future stressors.

While exercise is not a replacement for medication or therapy in the treatment of anxiety disorders, it can be a valuable addition to a comprehensive treatment plan. For people with mild to moderate anxiety symptoms, exercise may be enough to manage symptoms without the need for medication. For those with more severe symptoms, exercise can be a useful complement to medication and therapy.

So, what types of exercise are best for managing anxiety symptoms? The answer is that it depends on the individual. Any type of physical activity can be beneficial, as long as it is something that the person enjoys and is able to do regularly. Aerobic exercise, such as running, cycling, or swimming, has been found to be particularly effective in reducing anxiety symptoms.

However, other forms of exercise, such as yoga or weightlifting, can also be effective.

Strategies for implementing healthy habits

Anxiety disorders are the most common mental health disorders affecting millions of people worldwide. Anxiety can be a debilitating condition that affects a person's mental, emotional, and physical well-being. While there are many treatment options available, implementing healthy habits such as exercise and nutrition can be an effective way to manage anxiety symptoms. Below we will discuss the benefits of healthy habits and strategies for implementing them in daily life.

Firstly, let's discuss the role of diet and nutrition in managing anxiety symptoms. Research suggests that a healthy diet can have a positive impact on mental health. Eating a diet that is high in fruits, vegetables, whole grains, and lean proteins can help improve mood and reduce anxiety symptoms. In contrast, consuming a diet high in processed foods and sugar can have a negative impact on mental health. Such foods may lead to inflammation in the body, which can increase anxiety symptoms.

Some nutrients that are essential for mental health include omega-3 fatty acids, B vitamins, and magnesium. Omega-3 fatty acids are found in fatty fish such as salmon, sardines, and mackerel, and can help reduce inflammation in the body. B vitamins, found in whole grains, leafy greens, and meat, can help regulate mood and reduce stress. Magnesium, found in nuts, seeds, and leafy greens, can help promote relaxation and reduce anxiety symptoms.

In addition to a healthy diet, physical activity is another effective strategy for managing anxiety symptoms. Exercise has been shown to improve mood and reduce anxiety symptoms by releasing endorphins, which are feel-good chemicals in the brain. Regular exercise can also help improve sleep quality, which can be beneficial for people with anxiety disorders.

There are many different types of physical activity that can be effective for managing anxiety. Yoga, for example, has been shown to reduce symptoms of anxiety by promoting relaxation and mindfulness. Aerobic exercise such as running or cycling can also be effective for reducing anxiety symptoms. Resistance training, such as weightlifting, can help improve mood and reduce stress.

Now, let's discuss some strategies for implementing healthy habits in daily life. When it comes to diet and nutrition, it can be helpful to plan meals in advance and incorporate healthy snacks throughout the day. Keeping a food journal can also be a helpful tool for monitoring food intake and identifying triggers that may exacerbate anxiety symptoms. Additionally, avoiding caffeine and alcohol, which can exacerbate anxiety symptoms, can be beneficial.

When it comes to exercise, it can be helpful to set realistic goals and incorporate physical activity into daily routines. For example, taking a 30-minute walk after dinner or doing a yoga routine before bed can be effective ways to incorporate physical activity into daily life. It can also be helpful to find an exercise buddy or join a fitness class to stay motivated and accountable.

In addition to diet and exercise, it is important to practice good sleep hygiene to manage anxiety symptoms. This includes establishing a regular sleep schedule, avoiding electronic devices before bedtime, and creating a relaxing sleep environment. Additionally, relaxation techniques such as deep breathing, meditation, and progressive muscle relaxation can help promote relaxation and reduce anxiety symptoms.

Chapter Twenty-Five

Creative Expression and Anxiety

Creative expression refers to the use of various forms of art to communicate one's feelings and emotions. This can include anything from painting, writing, music, or even dance. While creative expression is often seen as a way to promote relaxation and reduce stress, it can also be a powerful tool in managing anxiety.

Anxiety disorders are characterized by persistent and excessive worry, fear, and/or panic. These symptoms can interfere with a person's ability to function in their daily life and can lead to avoidance behaviors that can make the anxiety worse over time. While traditional treatments such as medication and therapy can be effective in managing anxiety, there is growing evidence to suggest that creative expression can also be an important part of an anxiety management plan.

One of the benefits of creative expression is that it allows individuals to externalize their thoughts and feelings. Anxiety can often be an internal experience, with individuals feeling trapped in their own thoughts and emotions. By creating art, individuals can express these feelings in a concrete way, which can help to reduce the intensity of the emotions and provide a sense of relief.

Additionally, creative expression can be a form of mindfulness, which is a technique that involves focusing on the present moment and being aware of one's thoughts and emotions without judgment. By engaging in creative activities, individuals can enter into a state of flow, which is a state of deep concentration and engagement in an activity. This can provide a sense of calm and relaxation, which can be helpful in managing anxiety symptoms.

There are many different forms of creative expression that can be helpful in managing anxiety. For example, art therapy is a form of therapy that involves the use of various art forms, such as painting or drawing, to help individuals express and process their emotions. This can be particularly helpful for individuals who have difficulty expressing their emotions verbally.

Music therapy is another form of creative expression that can be helpful in managing anxiety. Music has been shown to have a powerful effect on emotions and can be used to promote relaxation and reduce stress. Additionally, playing music or singing can be a form of mindfulness, as it requires individuals to focus on the present moment and be fully engaged in the activity.

Writing is another form of creative expression that can be helpful in managing anxiety. Journaling, in particular, can be a powerful tool for individuals with anxiety. Writing down one's thoughts and feelings can help to externalize them and provide a sense of relief. Additionally, writing can be a form of self-reflection, which can help individuals to gain insight into their anxiety and develop strategies for managing it.

Dance and movement therapy is another form of creative expression that can be helpful in managing anxiety. Movement can be a powerful way to express emotions, and dance therapy can be used to help individuals connect with their bodies and release tension and stress.

While creative expression can be a powerful tool in managing anxiety, it is important to note that it is not a substitute for traditional treatments such as medication and therapy. Rather, it can be used as a complementary therapy to help individuals manage their anxiety symptoms.

Incorporating creative expression into one's daily routine can be a helpful way to manage anxiety. This can be as simple as taking a few minutes each day to engage in a creative activity, such as coloring or doodling. Additionally, seeking out opportunities to participate in structured creative activities, such as art or music therapy, can be a helpful way to incorporate creative expression into one's anxiety management plan.

The therapeutic potential of art, music, and writing

The experience of anxiety can be overwhelming, leaving individuals feeling lost and out of control. However, there are various therapeutic techniques that can help individuals cope with anxiety. One such technique is creative expression, which includes activities such as art, music, and writing. Creative expression allows individuals to explore their emotions and thoughts in a safe and constructive way, helping them better understand and manage their anxiety.

Art therapy is a form of therapy that uses creative expression as a tool for promoting emotional and mental well-being. It is often used in the treatment of anxiety disorders, as it allows individuals to express their emotions and feelings through visual art. Art therapy sessions may include activities such as drawing, painting, sculpting, and collage-making. By engaging in these activities, individuals can tap into their unconscious thoughts and feelings and express them in a tangible way. This can help individuals better understand and process their emotions, leading to reduced anxiety symptoms.

Music therapy is another form of creative expression that can be beneficial for individuals with anxiety disorders. It involves using music as a means of communication and expression, helping individuals to regulate their emotions and alleviate stress. Music therapy may include activities such as listening to music, singing, playing instruments, and composing music.

Studies have shown that music therapy can improve mood, reduce anxiety, and increase overall well-being in individuals with anxiety disorders.

Writing therapy is a form of therapy that involves using writing as a tool for exploring emotions and thoughts. It can be used to help individuals with anxiety disorders better understand and cope with their anxiety symptoms. Writing therapy may include activities such as journaling, creative writing, and poetry. By putting their thoughts and feelings down on paper, individuals can gain insight into their emotional state and develop a greater sense of self-awareness. Writing therapy has been found to be an effective tool for reducing anxiety symptoms and improving overall mental health.

In addition to promoting emotional and mental well-being, creative expression can also provide a sense of purpose and fulfillment. Engaging in creative activities can help individuals feel more connected to their inner selves, allowing them to tap into their personal strengths and abilities. It can also provide a sense of accomplishment, which can be particularly important for individuals struggling with anxiety.

There are various ways to incorporate creative expression into a daily routine. For example, individuals can set aside time each day to engage in an art project, play an instrument, or write in a journal. They can also attend group therapy sessions that focus on creative expression or seek out a therapist who specializes in creative therapies.

While creative expression can be a powerful tool for managing anxiety, it is important to remember that it is not a substitute for professional help. Individuals with anxiety disorders should seek out a qualified mental health professional for proper diagnosis and treatment. However, incorporating creative expression into a comprehensive treatment plan can be a valuable complement to traditional therapy and medication.

Strategies for channeling anxiety into creativity

Anxiety disorders can be debilitating, causing feelings of constant worry, fear, and panic. However, anxiety can also be channeled into a creative outlet. Creative expression can serve as a therapeutic tool to cope with anxiety and manage its symptoms. Below we will explore some strategies for channeling anxiety into creativity.

Art therapy is a form of therapy that uses the creative process to improve mental and emotional well-being. According to the American Art Therapy Association, art therapy can help individuals reduce anxiety, increase self-awareness, and improve their overall quality of life. Art therapy can be done with a professional art therapist, but it can also be done at home with simple materials such as paper and markers.

One way to channel anxiety into art is through creating a worry box. A worry box is a container, such as a shoebox, that is decorated with calming images and colors. Inside the box, individuals can write down their worries on slips of paper and place them inside the box. This activity can help individuals externalize their worries, making them more manageable.

Another form of creative expression is music therapy. Music therapy uses music to improve physical, emotional, cognitive, and social functioning. Studies have shown that music therapy can be an effective way to reduce anxiety symptoms.

Playing an instrument or singing can be a form of self-expression that can help individuals cope with anxiety. According to the Anxiety and Depression Association of America, listening to music can also be a helpful strategy for reducing anxiety symptoms. Listening to calming music, such as classical music or nature sounds, can help individuals relax and feel more at ease.

Writing can also be a powerful tool for managing anxiety symptoms. Journaling, for example, can help individuals express their thoughts and feelings in a safe and private way. This can be done in the form of a gratitude journal, where individuals write down things they are grateful for, or in the form of a worry journal, where individuals write down their worries and then try to reframe them in a more positive light.

Another form of writing is creative writing. Writing short stories, poems, or even a memoir can be a way to externalize thoughts and feelings about anxiety. Creative writing can also be used as a form of self-reflection, allowing individuals to gain insight into their anxiety triggers and patterns.

Incorporating physical activity into one's routine is also a helpful strategy for managing anxiety. According to the Anxiety and Depression Association of America, exercise can help reduce anxiety symptoms by releasing endorphins, which are chemicals in the brain that help improve mood.

Yoga, in particular, can be a helpful form of exercise for anxiety. Yoga incorporates physical postures, breathing exercises, and meditation, which can all help reduce anxiety symptoms. The focus on mindfulness and being present in the moment can also help individuals feel more grounded and less anxious.

Success stories of creative individuals with anxiety disorders

Anxiety disorders can be incredibly debilitating and can affect many aspects of a person's life, including their ability to be creative. However, some individuals with anxiety disorders have managed to channel their anxiety into their creative pursuits and have achieved great success. Below we will explore some success stories of creative individuals with anxiety disorders and how they were able to use their struggles with anxiety to fuel their creativity.

One of the most well-known examples of a successful creative individual with an anxiety disorder is the singer and songwriter, Adele. Adele has been open about her struggles with anxiety and panic attacks, and how they have affected her career. In an interview with Rolling Stone, she stated, "I have anxiety attacks, constant panicking on stage, my heart feels like it's going to explode because I never feel like I'm going to deliver, ever." Despite these struggles, Adele has achieved incredible success in her music career, with multiple Grammy Awards and record-breaking sales. Adele has said that her anxiety has actually helped her songwriting, stating, "It's a similar feeling to stage fright. You have to feel the fear and do it anyway, and write songs that are confessional, to be brave and honest and not care about what anyone thinks."

Another example of a successful creative individual with an anxiety disorder is the author John Green. Green has spoken openly about his struggles with anxiety and obsessive-compulsive disorder (OCD) and how they have affected his writing process. In an interview with The Guardian, Green stated, "It's incredibly frustrating to have OCD because it's like the obsessive part of your brain is making you do things that you don't want to do. But at the same time, I think it gives me a unique perspective on the world, and it's something that I can use in my writing." Green has achieved tremendous success as a young adult author, with his novels such as The Fault in Our Stars and Paper Towns becoming bestsellers and being adapted into successful films.

Another creative individual who has used their struggles with anxiety to fuel their creativity is the actor and comedian, Stephen Fry. Fry has been open about his struggles with bipolar disorder and how it has affected his life and career. In an interview with The Telegraph, Fry stated, "My bipolar disorder is a source of great creativity for me. It's a strange kind of alchemy, but the highs and lows I experience allow me to see the world in a different way and give me ideas for my work." Fry has achieved success in a variety of creative endeavors, including acting, writing, and comedy.

These success stories demonstrate that it is possible to channel anxiety into creativity and achieve great success. However, it is important to note that not everyone with an anxiety disorder will have the same experience. Anxiety can be incredibly debilitating and can interfere with a person's ability to be creative. Additionally, it is important for individuals with anxiety disorders to seek professional help if they are struggling to manage their symptoms.

Chapter Twenty-Six

Embracing Neurodiversity and Reducing Stigma

Embracing Neurodiversity and Reducing Stigma

Anxiety disorders are the most common mental health condition in the United States, affecting approximately 40 million adults each year. Despite the prevalence of anxiety disorders, stigma and misunderstanding still exist around the condition, often causing individuals to feel isolated and ashamed of their struggles. However, a growing movement towards neurodiversity is helping to reduce this stigma and promote a more inclusive understanding of mental health.

Neurodiversity is the concept that individuals with neurological differences, including those with anxiety disorders, should be embraced for their unique perspectives and abilities, rather than stigmatized for their differences. This approach recognizes that neurological diversity is a natural and valuable aspect of human variation, and that individuals with anxiety disorders can make meaningful contributions to society.

By embracing neurodiversity, we can reduce the stigma associated with anxiety disorders and promote greater understanding and acceptance of those with the condition. This can lead to increased social support and improved mental health outcomes for individuals with anxiety disorders.

One way to embrace neurodiversity is through education and awareness-raising. Many people are unaware of the reality of anxiety disorders and may hold stigmatizing beliefs about those who experience anxiety.

By educating the public about the causes, symptoms, and treatments of anxiety disorders, we can increase understanding and reduce the stigma surrounding the condition.

Another way to embrace neurodiversity is by promoting self-advocacy and empowerment for individuals with anxiety disorders. This means encouraging individuals with anxiety to speak openly about their experiences and advocating for their own needs in various settings, such as in the workplace or in social situations. By doing so, individuals can break down barriers and challenge negative stereotypes associated with anxiety disorders.

Furthermore, it is important to recognize the unique strengths and abilities of individuals with anxiety disorders. Many people with anxiety are highly empathetic, detail-oriented, and creative, and these traits can be valuable in many contexts. By recognizing and celebrating these strengths, we can promote a more inclusive and positive understanding of anxiety disorders.

While there is still much work to be done in reducing the stigma surrounding anxiety disorders, the neurodiversity movement provides a hopeful path forward. By embracing the unique perspectives and abilities of individuals with anxiety, we can create a more inclusive and accepting society for all.

The importance of understanding and accepting mental health differences

The human brain is one of the most complex and intricate organs in the human body, and as such, it can exhibit a wide range of variations and differences. These differences in brain structure and function can give rise to different ways of thinking, processing information, and responding to different stimuli. In recent years, there has been a growing recognition of the importance of neurodiversity, which refers to the wide range of differences in brain function and behavior that are considered natural variations in the human population.

However, despite the growing awareness of the importance of neurodiversity, there is still a lot of stigma surrounding mental health differences, such as anxiety disorders. Anxiety disorders are a type of mental health condition that is characterized by feelings of fear, worry, and nervousness that can be difficult to control or manage. These feelings can be intense and long-lasting, and they can interfere with daily activities and relationships.

One of the main reasons why there is still a lot of stigma surrounding mental health differences is that they are often not well understood. For example, many people might not realize that anxiety disorders are not just a result of a person being weak-willed or lacking in self-control. Rather, anxiety disorders are complex conditions that involve a variety of biological, psychological, and environmental factors.

In addition, there is often a tendency to view mental health differences as negative or undesirable. For example, a person with an anxiety disorder might be seen as being overly anxious or nervous, which can lead to negative attitudes and judgments. This can create a sense of shame and embarrassment for individuals with anxiety disorders, which can make it difficult for them to seek help and support.

However, it is important to recognize that anxiety disorders are just one form of neurodiversity, and that there are many other ways in which the brain can exhibit differences. For example, some people may have a more introverted personality, while others may have a more extroverted personality. Some people may have a higher degree of sensitivity to certain types of sensory input, while others may have a higher degree of resistance.

Ultimately, what is important is to recognize and accept these differences as natural variations in the human population. Rather than seeing anxiety disorders or other mental health conditions as something negative or undesirable, we should strive to create an environment in which these differences are accepted and celebrated.

One way to reduce stigma and promote acceptance of neurodiversity is through education and awareness. By learning more about anxiety disorders and other mental health conditions, we can begin to understand the complexity and variability of the human brain, and we can develop a greater appreciation for the diversity of human experience.

Another important step is to provide support and resources for individuals with anxiety disorders and other mental health conditions. This can include access to mental health professionals, support groups, and other resources that can help individuals manage their symptoms and live fulfilling lives.

Finally, we can all play a role in reducing stigma and promoting acceptance by treating individuals with mental health differences with respect and empathy. This means being mindful of the language we use when talking about mental health, avoiding stereotypes and negative attitudes, and recognizing that everyone has unique strengths and challenges.

Challenging stigma and misconceptions about anxiety disorders

Anxiety disorders are a prevalent mental health condition that affects millions of people worldwide. Despite the high prevalence, anxiety disorders continue to be stigmatized and misunderstood by many. It is important to challenge these stigmas and misconceptions in order to increase awareness and understanding of anxiety disorders.

One of the most common misconceptions about anxiety disorders is that they are not a real medical condition. Many people believe that individuals with anxiety disorders are simply overreacting or being dramatic. However, anxiety disorders are a legitimate medical condition that affects the brain and body. Anxiety disorders can cause physical symptoms such as headaches, nausea, and fatigue, as well as emotional symptoms such as excessive worry, fear, and avoidance.

Another misconception about anxiety disorders is that they are simply a sign of weakness or personal failure. In reality, anxiety disorders are not caused by personal weakness or lack of willpower. They are caused by a combination of genetic, environmental, and psychological factors. Anyone can develop an anxiety disorder, regardless of their background, personality, or strength.

There is also a misconception that anxiety disorders are rare and only affect a small portion of the population. However, anxiety disorders are actually one of the most common mental health conditions worldwide. In fact, approximately 1 in 5 adults in the United States experience an anxiety disorder each year. Despite the high prevalence, many people with anxiety disorders do not seek treatment due to the stigma surrounding mental illness.

Stigmatizing attitudes towards anxiety disorders can have serious consequences for those who suffer from them. Stigma can make individuals with anxiety disorders feel ashamed or embarrassed about their condition, and may discourage them from seeking treatment. This can lead to a worsening of symptoms and decreased quality of life.

Challenging stigma and misconceptions about anxiety disorders is essential in order to reduce the negative impact of these attitudes. Education and awareness campaigns can help to increase understanding of anxiety disorders and reduce the fear and stigma surrounding them. These campaigns can include public service announcements, community events, and online resources that provide accurate information about anxiety disorders.

It is also important to recognize the diversity within the anxiety disorder community. Anxiety disorders can manifest differently in different individuals, and each person's experience is unique. This diversity should be celebrated and embraced, rather than stigmatized or overlooked. This concept is known as neurodiversity, which recognizes the value of different neurological conditions and perspectives.

In addition to education and awareness campaigns, reducing stigma towards anxiety disorders can also be achieved through increased representation in media and entertainment. Portrayals of individuals with anxiety disorders in TV shows, movies, and books can help to reduce the negative stereotypes associated with anxiety disorders and provide a more accurate portrayal of the experiences of those with anxiety.

Reducing stigma towards anxiety disorders can have a significant impact on the lives of those who suffer from them. It can help to reduce the fear and shame associated with seeking treatment and increase the likelihood that individuals will seek out the help they need. This can lead to improved mental health outcomes and a better quality of life for those with anxiety disorders.

Advocating for a more inclusive and supportive society

Anxiety disorders are a common mental health condition affecting millions of people worldwide. Yet, despite the prevalence of anxiety disorders, individuals with anxiety often face stigmatization and misconceptions about their condition. Challenging and overcoming stigma is crucial to creating a more inclusive and supportive society for those living with anxiety disorders.

One of the biggest challenges for individuals with anxiety disorders is the misconception that anxiety is a weakness or a character flaw. Many people with anxiety disorders may feel shame and guilt about their symptoms, leading them to avoid seeking help or support. It is crucial to understand that anxiety disorders are a legitimate medical condition and not a personal failing.

Another misconception about anxiety disorders is that they are not severe enough to require professional treatment. Anxiety disorders can significantly impact an individual's daily life, relationships, and overall well-being. Seeking professional help, such as therapy or medication, is an essential step in managing anxiety disorders.

Stigma and misconceptions can also lead to social isolation for individuals with anxiety disorders. Fear of being judged or misunderstood can cause individuals to avoid social situations, leading to feelings of loneliness and depression. Creating a more inclusive and supportive society involves creating safe spaces where individuals with anxiety disorders feel comfortable and accepted.

There are several ways to challenge stigma and advocate for a more inclusive society. One of the most effective ways is by increasing public awareness and understanding of anxiety disorders. This can involve sharing personal stories and experiences, creating educational materials, and participating in community events and discussions.

Another way to challenge stigma is by promoting a language of empathy and compassion. Using derogatory language or dismissing anxiety symptoms can perpetuate stigmatization and make it harder for individuals with anxiety disorders to seek help. Instead, using language that reflects empathy and understanding can help break down barriers and create a more supportive environment.

Advocating for systemic change is also crucial in creating a more inclusive and supportive society for individuals with anxiety disorders. This can involve advocating for policies that prioritize mental health, increasing funding for mental health research, and increasing access to affordable mental health care.

Ultimately, challenging stigma and misconceptions about anxiety disorders is essential in creating a more inclusive and supportive society. By promoting understanding, empathy, and systemic change, we can break down barriers and provide support for individuals with anxiety disorders to live healthy and fulfilling lives.

Chapter Twenty-Seven

Resources and Support Networks

Anxiety disorders are a common mental health condition affecting millions of people worldwide. It is a condition that can severely impact an individual's quality of life, making it challenging to maintain relationships, work, and other important aspects of daily life. However, there are many resources and support networks available to help individuals with anxiety disorders manage their symptoms and improve their overall wellbeing.

One of the most significant resources for individuals with anxiety disorders is mental health professionals. These professionals are trained to diagnose and treat anxiety disorders, providing therapy, medication, and other forms of treatment. There are different types of mental health professionals available, including psychologists, psychiatrists, social workers, and counselors. They can help individuals with anxiety disorders develop coping strategies and provide support throughout their recovery process.

Additionally, there are various support groups available for individuals with anxiety disorders. These groups are designed to provide a safe and supportive environment for individuals to share their experiences, connect with others, and learn from each other. Support groups can be in-person or online, and there are many different types of groups available, including those for specific anxiety disorders and those for individuals of different ages and backgrounds.

In recent years, there has been a significant increase in the availability of online resources for individuals with anxiety disorders. There are many websites, forums, and online communities designed to provide information, support, and resources to individuals with anxiety disorders. These online resources can be an excellent option for those who are unable to attend in-person support groups or seek treatment due to financial or other barriers.

There are also many self-help resources available for individuals with anxiety disorders. These resources include books, workbooks, apps, and online courses designed to provide individuals with the tools and strategies they need to manage their anxiety symptoms. Self-help resources can be an excellent option for individuals who prefer to manage their symptoms independently or who are unable to access traditional forms of treatment.

Aside from mental health professionals and support networks, there are also many lifestyle changes and practices individuals with anxiety disorders can adopt to improve their overall wellbeing. These lifestyle changes include regular exercise, healthy eating habits, getting enough sleep, and practicing relaxation techniques such as yoga and meditation. These practices can help reduce stress and anxiety levels, promoting a better quality of life.

Finding professional help and support

Anxiety disorders are a common mental health condition that affects millions of people worldwide. While many individuals can manage their symptoms with self-care techniques, some may require professional help and support. Finding the right treatment can be a challenge, but there are resources and support networks available to those who need them.

One of the first steps in finding professional help for anxiety is to talk to a healthcare provider. Primary care physicians, mental health professionals, and psychiatrists can all provide assessments and treatment options for individuals with anxiety. They may prescribe medication, therapy, or a combination of both, depending on the severity of the symptoms.

Therapy is often recommended for individuals with anxiety disorders, as it can help individuals learn coping mechanisms and address the underlying causes of their anxiety. There are several types of therapy that may be helpful, including cognitive-behavioral therapy (CBT), exposure therapy, and mindfulness-based therapy. CBT is a commonly used therapy that focuses on identifying negative thought patterns and replacing them with more positive and realistic ones. Exposure therapy involves gradually exposing the individual to the source of their anxiety in a controlled and safe environment. Mindfulness-based therapy focuses on cultivating mindfulness and awareness of the present moment to help reduce anxiety symptoms.

Support groups can also be a valuable resource for individuals with anxiety. These groups provide a space for individuals to connect with others who share similar experiences and provide emotional support. There are both online and in-person support groups available, and they can be found through organizations like the National Alliance on Mental Illness (NAMI) or Anxiety and Depression Association of America (ADAA).

In addition to professional help and support groups, there are also self-care techniques that individuals with anxiety can use to manage their symptoms. These include regular exercise, practicing relaxation techniques like deep breathing and meditation, getting enough sleep, and eating a healthy and balanced diet. Avoiding triggers like caffeine, alcohol, and nicotine can also be helpful for managing anxiety symptoms.

There are also several resources available online for individuals with anxiety. The ADAA and NAMI both offer resources and information on anxiety disorders, as well as online support groups and treatment directories. The Anxiety and Depression Association of America also offers a resource center for finding mental health professionals, including therapists, psychiatrists, and support groups.

Teletherapy has also become an increasingly popular option for individuals with anxiety, particularly during the COVID-19 pandemic. Many mental health professionals now offer virtual therapy sessions, which can be accessed from the comfort of one's own home. This can be a convenient and accessible option for those who may have difficulty accessing traditional in-person therapy.

It's important to remember that seeking help for anxiety is a sign of strength, not weakness. Mental health conditions, including anxiety, are common and treatable. With the right support and resources, individuals with anxiety can manage their symptoms and lead fulfilling lives.

Connecting with others through support groups and online communities

Anxiety disorders affect millions of people worldwide and can be a challenging experience to navigate alone. The good news is that there are many resources and support networks available for those struggling with anxiety. Support groups and online communities can offer a safe and non-judgmental space for individuals to connect with others who are experiencing similar challenges. Below we will explore the benefits of connecting with others through support groups and online communities for those with anxiety disorders.

Support groups are an excellent resource for individuals with anxiety disorders. They offer a chance for individuals to connect with others who understand their struggles and offer support and encouragement. Support groups are often led by trained professionals or individuals with lived experience with anxiety disorders. They provide a safe and confidential space for members to share their experiences and learn from others. Members can gain a sense of community, which can be helpful in reducing feelings of isolation and loneliness.

One benefit of attending a support group is the opportunity to learn coping strategies from others who have similar experiences. Members can share what has worked for them and provide practical advice on how to manage anxiety symptoms. This information can be invaluable, especially for individuals who are newly diagnosed with an anxiety disorder. Members can also receive validation for their experiences, which can help reduce the shame and stigma often associated with mental health conditions.

In addition to in-person support groups, online communities can also be a valuable resource for individuals with anxiety disorders. Online communities can provide access to support 24/7, which is helpful for those who may need assistance outside of traditional business hours. Online communities can also offer anonymity, which can be helpful for individuals who may not feel comfortable sharing their experiences in-person. Members can connect with others from all over the world, which can provide a sense of universality in the experience of anxiety.

Online communities can be found on social media platforms, such as Facebook or Twitter, or on websites dedicated to mental health. Many organizations offer online support groups and forums where individuals can connect with others who have similar experiences. These communities can also provide access to resources and information about anxiety disorders, such as treatment options and self-care strategies.

It is essential to note that online communities may not be a suitable option for everyone. Some individuals may prefer in-person support groups or may not have access to the internet. It is crucial to find a support network that works best for the individual's needs.

One of the most significant benefits of support groups and online communities is the sense of community they provide. Individuals with anxiety disorders may feel isolated and alone, but connecting with others who understand their experiences can provide a sense of belonging. Members can provide emotional support, encouragement, and validation, which can be helpful in reducing symptoms of anxiety. The sense of community can also be a motivating factor in seeking treatment and making positive changes in one's life.

Accessing educational materials and resources

Anxiety disorders are a common mental health condition that affects millions of people worldwide. It is characterized by intense feelings of fear, worry, and unease, often triggered by specific situations or objects. Although anxiety disorders are highly treatable, accessing educational materials and resources is essential to help individuals manage their symptoms and lead fulfilling lives.

There are numerous resources available that provide valuable information on anxiety disorders. One of the most reliable sources is the National Institute of Mental Health (NIMH), which offers comprehensive resources on various mental health conditions, including anxiety disorders. The NIMH website contains detailed information about different types of anxiety disorders, their symptoms, causes, and treatments. The website also provides links to other resources, such as support groups and treatment facilities.

The Anxiety and Depression Association of America (ADAA) is another organization that provides resources for individuals struggling with anxiety disorders. Their website offers information on different types of anxiety disorders, treatment options, and coping strategies. The ADAA also provides a searchable directory of mental health professionals, making it easier for individuals to find a therapist or psychiatrist in their area who specializes in treating anxiety disorders.

In addition to these resources, many books and self-help guides are available that can be beneficial for individuals with anxiety disorders. One example is the book "The Anxiety and Phobia Workbook" by Edmund J. Bourne. This book offers practical exercises and techniques for managing anxiety symptoms, as well as information on different types of anxiety disorders and their treatments. Another helpful book is "Rewire Your Anxious Brain" by Catherine Pittman and Elizabeth Karle, which offers insights into the brain mechanisms behind anxiety and practical strategies for managing anxious thoughts and behaviors.

For individuals who prefer online resources, there are numerous websites and apps that can help manage anxiety symptoms. One example is the app Headspace, which offers guided meditations and mindfulness exercises to help manage anxiety and stress. Another app is Sanvello, which provides tools for tracking moods, setting goals, and accessing cognitive-behavioral therapy exercises. Online communities and forums, such as Reddit's Anxiety community, can also provide support and advice from individuals who have similar experiences with anxiety disorders.

Accessing educational materials and resources is critical for individuals with anxiety disorders to manage their symptoms and improve their quality of life. However, it is important to note that these resources are not a substitute for professional medical advice and treatment. If you are struggling with anxiety symptoms, it is essential to seek professional help from a licensed mental health provider. With the right resources and support, individuals with anxiety disorders can learn to manage their symptoms and lead fulfilling lives.

Chapter Twenty-Eight

Personal Stories and Experiences

Anxiety disorders affect millions of people worldwide, with various causes and symptoms. Many people suffer from anxiety in silence, but in recent years, there has been a growing movement of individuals sharing their personal experiences with anxiety to reduce stigma and promote understanding.

Personal stories and experiences can be powerful tools in raising awareness about anxiety disorders. They can help individuals recognize that they are not alone in their struggles and provide a sense of validation for their feelings. Personal stories can also be a source of hope for those who are struggling, showing that it is possible to manage anxiety and lead a fulfilling life.

Sharing personal stories can also help break down stigma surrounding anxiety disorders. Stigma often arises from a lack of understanding and misinformation about mental health. By sharing their experiences, individuals with anxiety can help educate others and combat stigma. By opening up about their struggles, individuals can inspire others to seek help and reduce feelings of shame or embarrassment.

Furthermore, personal stories can provide insight into the challenges and triumphs of living with anxiety. They can illustrate the different types of anxiety disorders, their symptoms, and how they impact daily life. This understanding can be helpful for both individuals who are experiencing anxiety themselves and those who are supporting someone with anxiety.

Personal stories can also provide insight into the various treatments and coping strategies that can help manage anxiety. They can highlight the effectiveness of therapies such as cognitive-behavioral therapy, mindfulness, and medication. They can also demonstrate how lifestyle changes, such as exercise, diet, and stress management, can have a positive impact on mental health.

Moreover, sharing personal stories can create a sense of community and support for individuals with anxiety. Support groups and online communities allow individuals to connect with others who share similar experiences, providing a safe space for individuals to share their thoughts and feelings. It can also provide a sense of belonging and a reminder that individuals with anxiety are not alone in their struggles.

Insights from individuals living with anxiety disorders

Anxiety disorders are among the most common mental health conditions, affecting millions of people worldwide. While anxiety can be a normal part of life, excessive and persistent anxiety can interfere with daily functioning and lead to significant distress. Anxiety disorders can manifest in different ways, such as generalized anxiety disorder, panic disorder, social anxiety disorder, and specific phobias. People with anxiety disorders may experience symptoms such as excessive worrying, panic attacks, avoidance behavior, and physical symptoms like sweating, trembling, and racing heart.

Living with anxiety disorders can be challenging, but many individuals have found ways to cope and manage their symptoms effectively. Insights from these individuals can provide valuable perspectives on what it's like to live with anxiety and how to navigate the challenges that come with it.

One insight that many people with anxiety disorders share is the importance of self-care. Taking care of oneself physically, emotionally, and mentally can help manage anxiety symptoms and improve overall well-being. This includes getting enough sleep, eating a balanced diet, exercising regularly, practicing relaxation techniques like deep breathing or meditation, and seeking professional help when needed.

Another important insight is the value of support from others. Living with anxiety disorders can feel isolating and overwhelming, but connecting with others who share similar experiences can be helpful. Support groups, online forums, and counseling services can provide a safe space to discuss challenges and receive emotional support. Some people also find that talking openly with family and friends about their anxiety can help reduce stigma and increase understanding.

Many people with anxiety disorders also find that engaging in creative activities can help alleviate symptoms. Art, music, and writing can serve as a form of self-expression and provide a sense of control and mastery. Some people find that creative pursuits help them relax and enter a state of flow, which can be calming and soothing.

Finally, it's important to recognize that living with anxiety disorders is a process of ongoing learning and growth. It's okay to make mistakes, experience setbacks, and struggle at times. Accepting oneself and one's experiences without judgment can help cultivate a sense of self-compassion and resilience. Many people with anxiety disorders find that they are able to live fulfilling lives and achieve their goals, even while managing their symptoms.

Overcoming challenges and celebrating successes

Anxiety disorders can present significant challenges in daily life. The experience of living with anxiety can feel isolating and overwhelming, with fear and worry often dominating one's thoughts and actions. However, with the right support and resources, individuals can overcome the challenges posed by anxiety and celebrate their successes.

One key to overcoming anxiety is developing effective coping strategies. Coping strategies can include mindfulness, exercise, nutrition, and creative expression, among others. Mindfulness practices such as meditation, deep breathing, and yoga can help individuals to calm their minds and bodies, reducing the impact of anxiety symptoms. Exercise has been shown to have a positive effect on mental health, reducing symptoms of anxiety and depression. A healthy diet can also contribute to better mental health, as certain foods have been shown to impact mood and anxiety levels.

Creative expression can also be an effective coping strategy for individuals with anxiety. Art, music, and writing can provide an outlet for self-expression and can be a therapeutic way to process difficult emotions. For example, painting or drawing can be a way to express emotions without having to put them into words, while writing can help individuals to process and reflect on their experiences.

In addition to developing coping strategies, seeking out support is essential for managing anxiety. Support can come from a variety of sources, including friends and family, support groups, and mental health professionals. Support groups and online communities can provide individuals with a sense of community and a safe space to share their experiences and emotions. Mental health professionals can offer personalized treatment plans, including therapy and medication, to address the specific needs of each individual.

Personal stories and experiences can also provide valuable insights into living with anxiety. Hearing from others who have experienced similar challenges can provide a sense of validation and hope, and can help individuals to feel less alone. Hearing about the strategies that others have used to manage their anxiety can also provide inspiration and ideas for new coping strategies.

Despite the challenges posed by anxiety disorders, individuals can celebrate their successes along the way. Successes can include small victories, such as facing a fear or trying a new coping strategy, or larger accomplishments, such as achieving a goal or overcoming a major challenge. Celebrating successes can help to build confidence and resilience, and can provide motivation to continue working towards recovery.

However, it is important to recognize that recovery from anxiety disorders is not a linear process. There may be setbacks and challenges along the way, and it is important to approach recovery with patience and self-compassion. Celebrating successes can be a reminder of the progress that has been made, even in the face of setbacks.

Inspiring stories of resilience and courage

Anxiety disorders are a common mental health condition that affects millions of people worldwide. While anxiety can be debilitating, many individuals have found ways to manage their symptoms and live fulfilling lives. Below we will explore some inspiring stories of resilience and courage in the face of anxiety.

One such story is that of Emma Stone, a Hollywood actress known for her roles in movies like La La Land and The Help. Stone has been open about her struggles with anxiety, including panic attacks and social anxiety. In an interview with Rolling Stone, she spoke about how acting has helped her manage her anxiety, stating that "It gave me a sense of purpose, made me feel less alone, made me feel like I belonged somewhere."

Another inspiring story is that of John Green, a best-selling author of books like The Fault in Our Stars and Turtles All the Way Down. Green has also been open about his struggles with anxiety and obsessive-compulsive disorder (OCD), and has used his platform to raise awareness about mental health. In an interview with Time magazine, he spoke about how writing has helped him cope with his anxiety, stating that "When I'm writing, I can forget everything else."

In addition to celebrities, many ordinary individuals have also overcome their anxiety and found ways to thrive. One such person is Sarah Wilson, an Australian author and entrepreneur who has been open about her struggles with anxiety and bipolar disorder. Wilson has used her platform to advocate for mental health and to encourage others to seek help. In an interview with The Guardian, she spoke about how she has learned to manage her anxiety through mindfulness practices and exercise.

Another inspiring story is that of Tanya J. Peterson, an author and speaker who has written extensively about her experiences with anxiety and panic disorder. Peterson has used her personal experiences to help others, speaking at conferences and writing books on mental health. In an interview with Psych Central, she spoke about how she has learned to manage her anxiety through therapy, medication, and self-care practices like meditation.

These individuals and many others have shown that it is possible to live a fulfilling life with anxiety. While managing anxiety can be a daily struggle, there are many strategies and resources available to help individuals cope. From therapy and medication to mindfulness practices and creative expression, there is no one-size-fits-all approach to managing anxiety.

However, by being open about their experiences and sharing their stories, these individuals have helped reduce stigma surrounding mental health and inspire others to seek help.

9781776968701
SD - #0032 - 140926 - C0 - 229/152/14 - PB - 9781776968701 - Matt Lamination